This book belongs to:

....

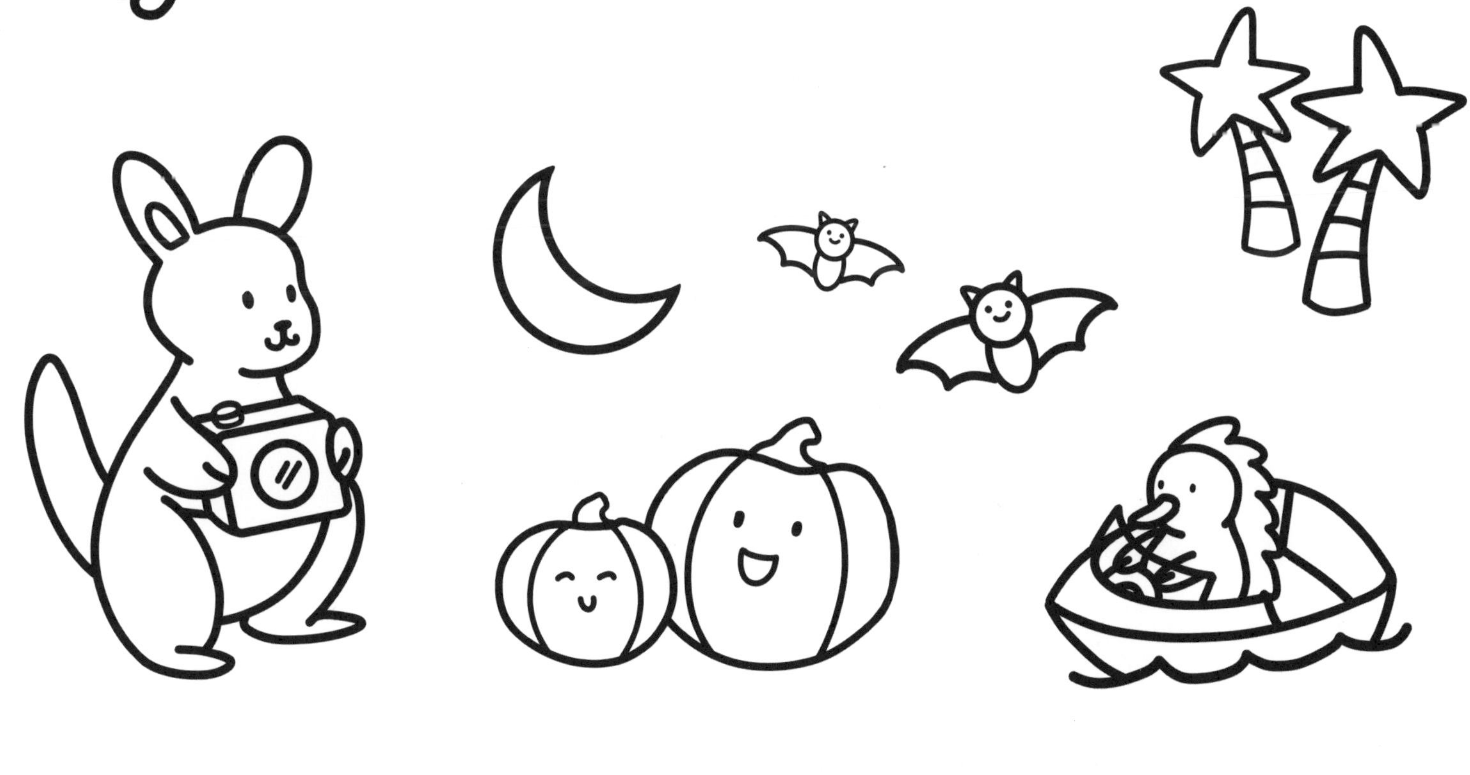

First published by Albert Street Books, an imprint of Allen & Unwin, in 2025

Allen & Unwin
Cammeraygal Country
83 Alexander Street
Crows Nest NSW 2065
Australia
Phone: (61 2) 8425 0100
Email: info@allenandunwin.com
Web: www.allenandunwin.com

Allen & Unwin acknowledges the Traditional Owners of the Country on which we live and work.
We pay our respects to all Aboriginal and Torres Strait Islander Elders, past and present.

EU Authorised Representative: Easy Access System Europe,
Mustamäe tee 50, 10621 Tallinn, Estonia, gpsr.requests@easproject.com

A catalogue record for this book is available from the National Library of Australia

ISBN 978 1 76118 257 0

For teaching resources, explore allenandunwin.com/learn

Cover and text design by Hana Kinoshita Thomson
Set in 16 pt Noyh R Regular by Hana Kinoshita Thomson
Printed in September 2025 by C&C Offset Printing Co. Ltd, China

10 9 8 7 6 5 4 3 2

MIX
Paper | Supporting responsible forestry
FSC® C008047

HELLO HOLIDAYS

cosy Aussie colouring

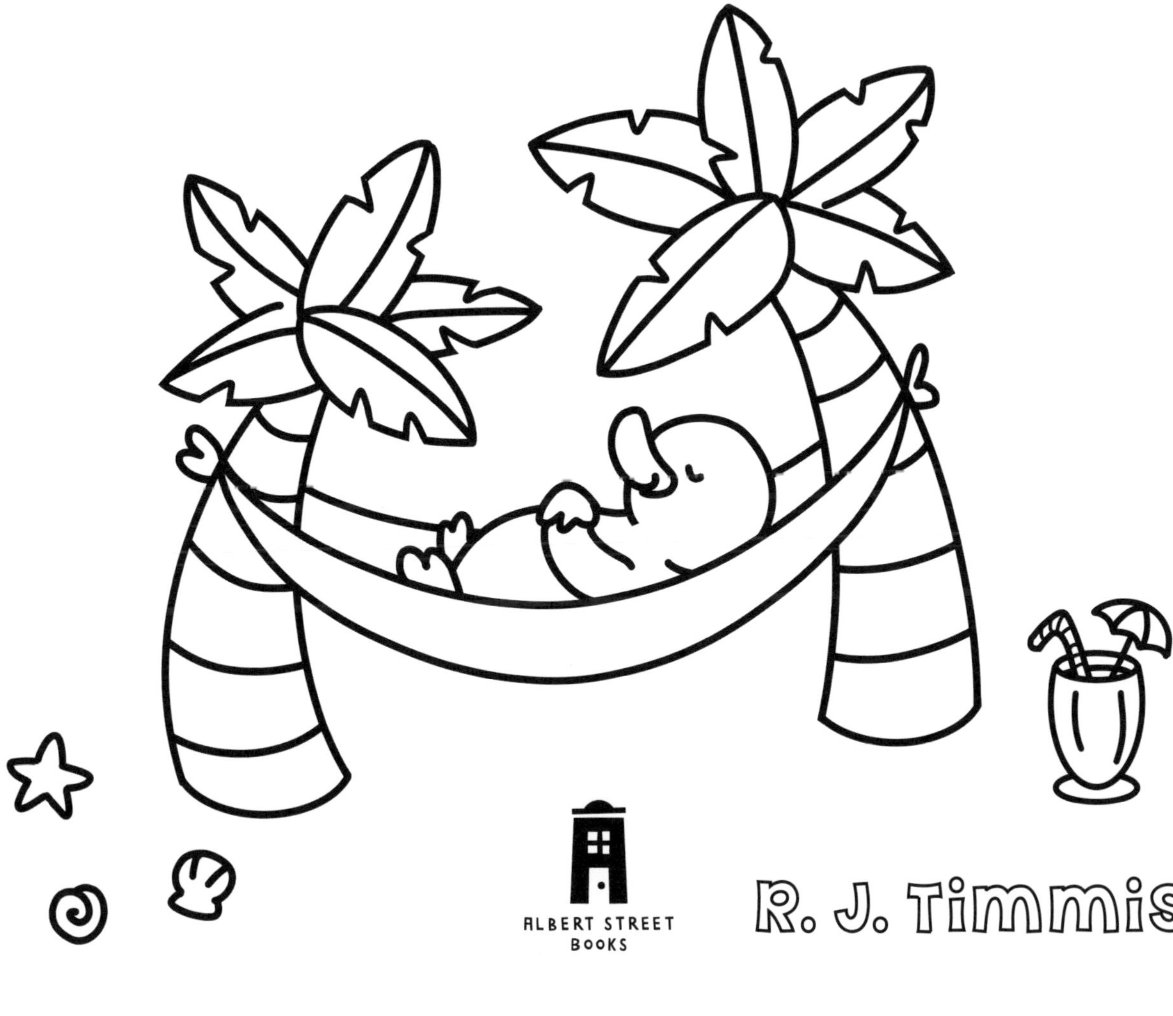

ALBERT STREET BOOKS

R. J. Timmis

HELLO, FRIEND!

Colouring is a great way to slow down, clear your mind and enjoy a little creative me-time. So, find a comfy spot, grab your favourite colouring tools and let the fun begin!

BEFORE YOU START

You can use the very first page of this book to test your markers, colour pencils or crayons.

Don't forget to place a piece of card or thick paper behind the page you're working on to protect the next illustration.

HAPPY COLOURING!

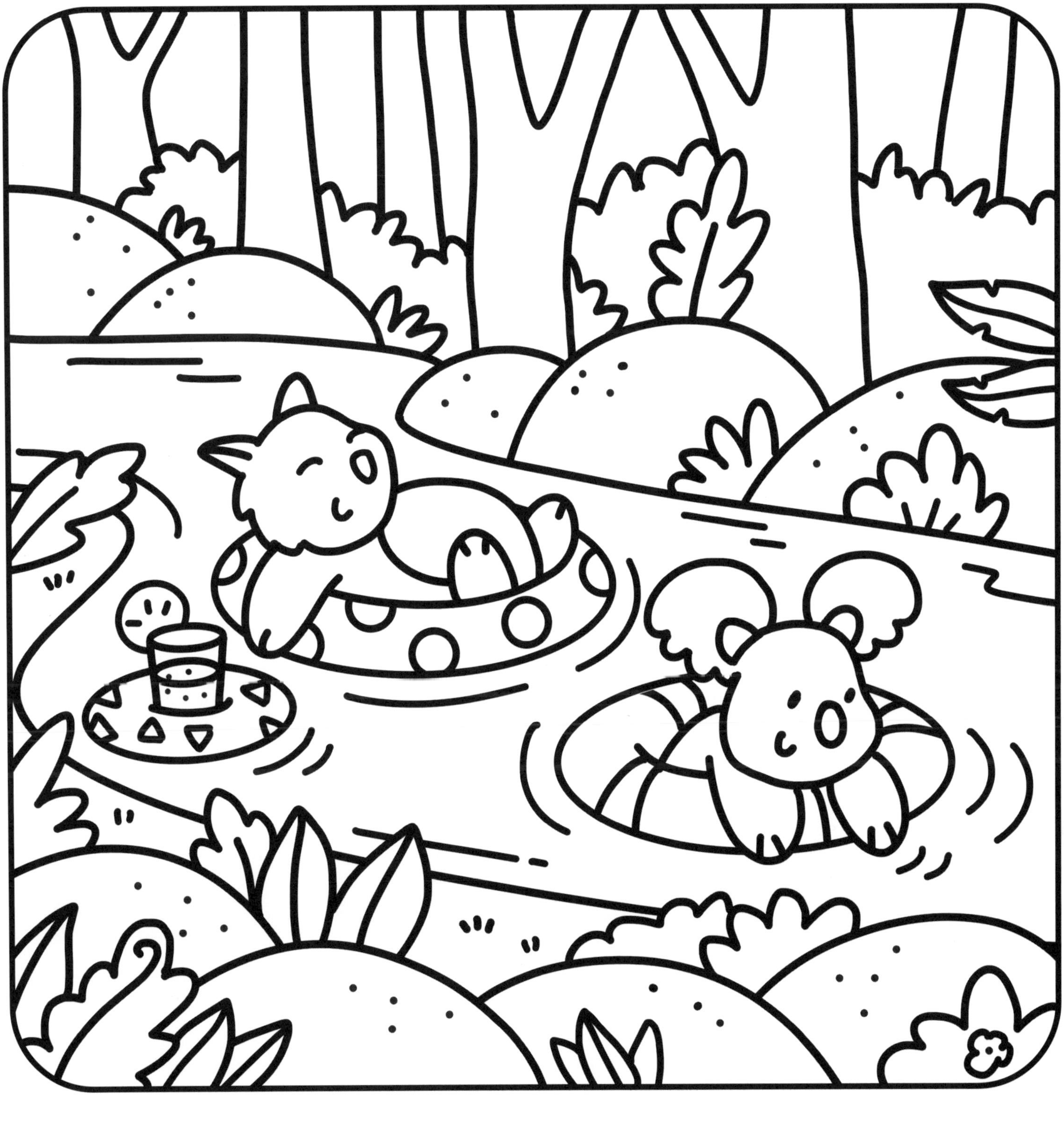

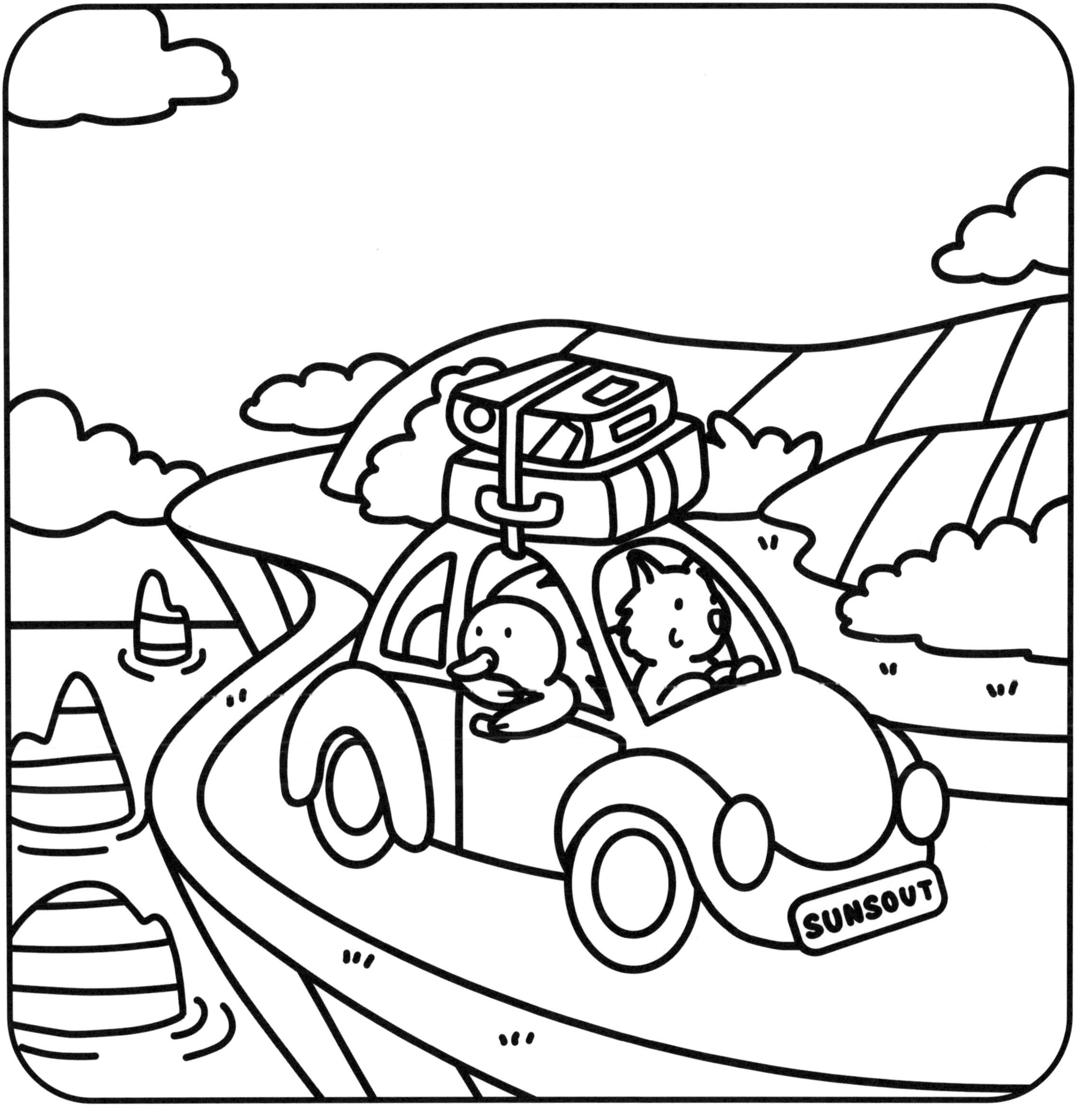
SUNSOUT

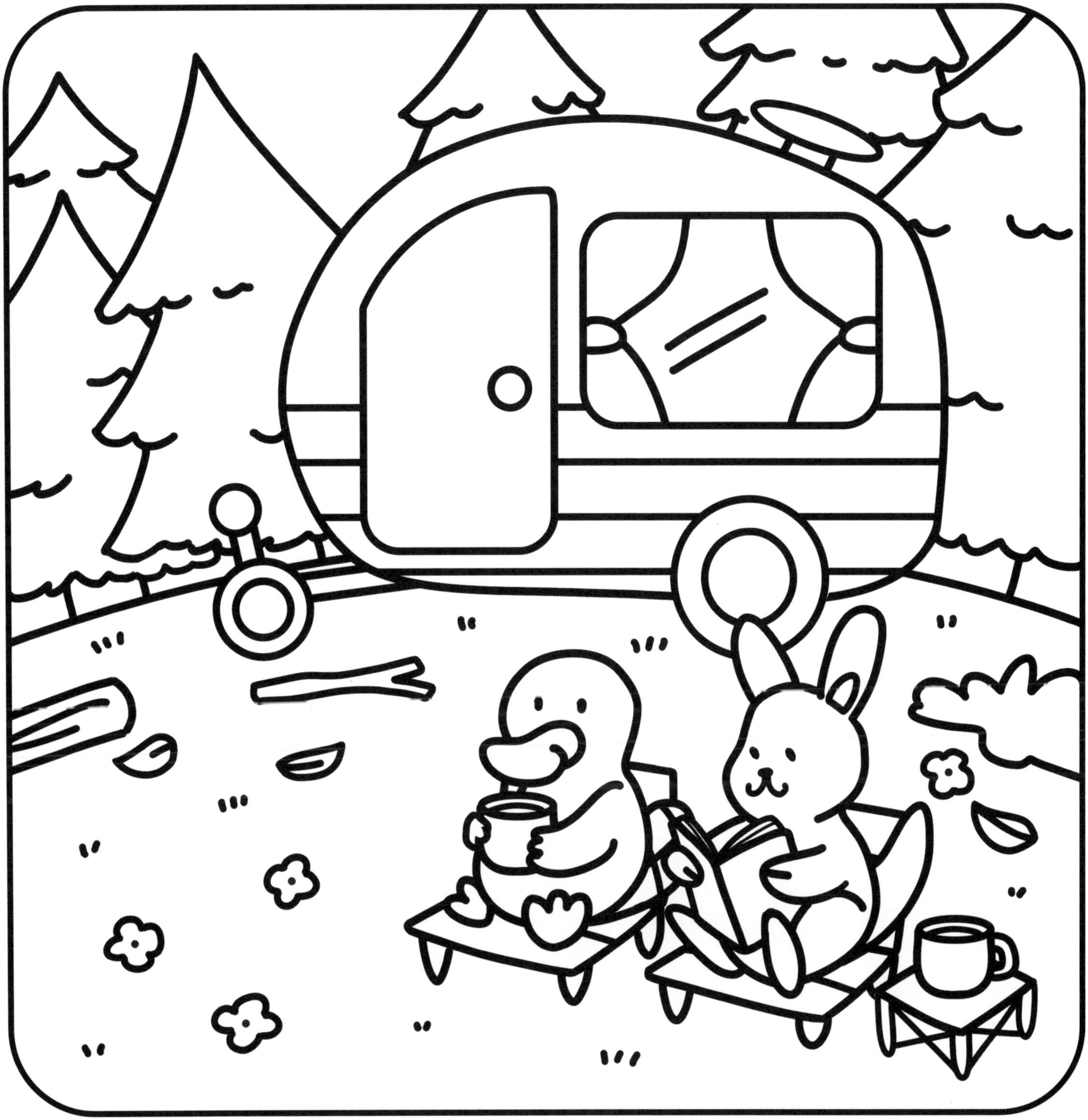

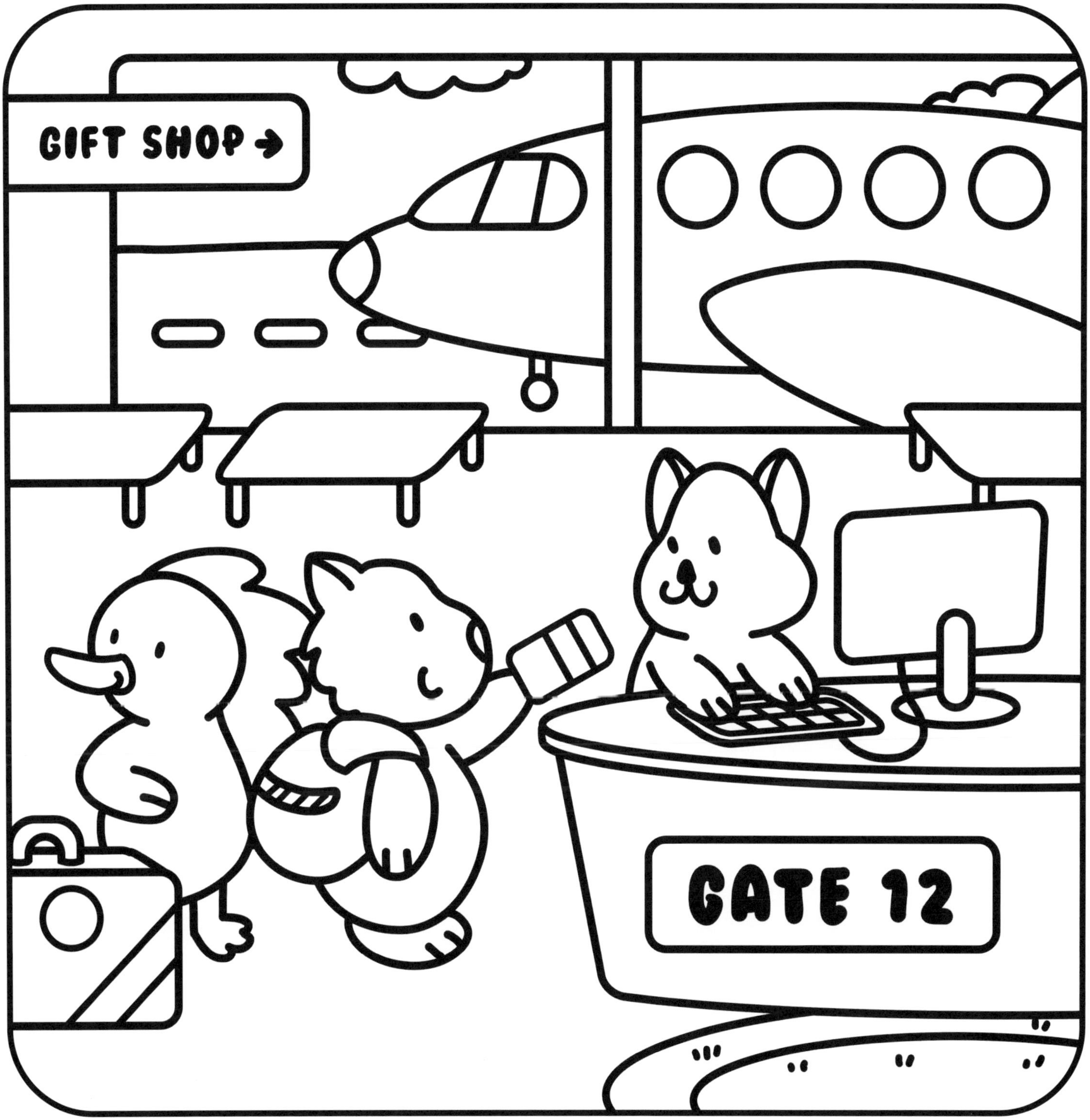
GIFT SHOP →
GATE 12

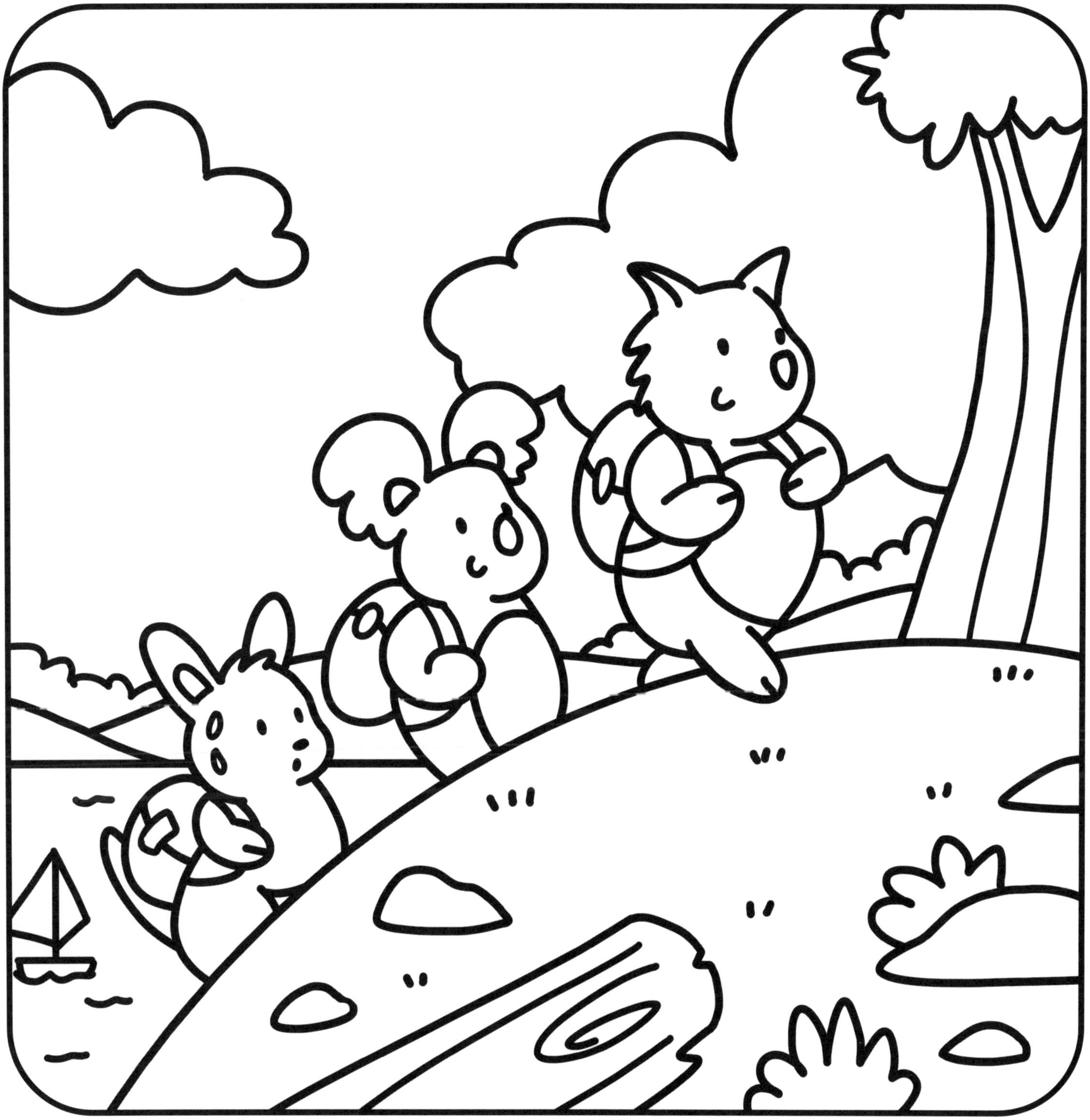

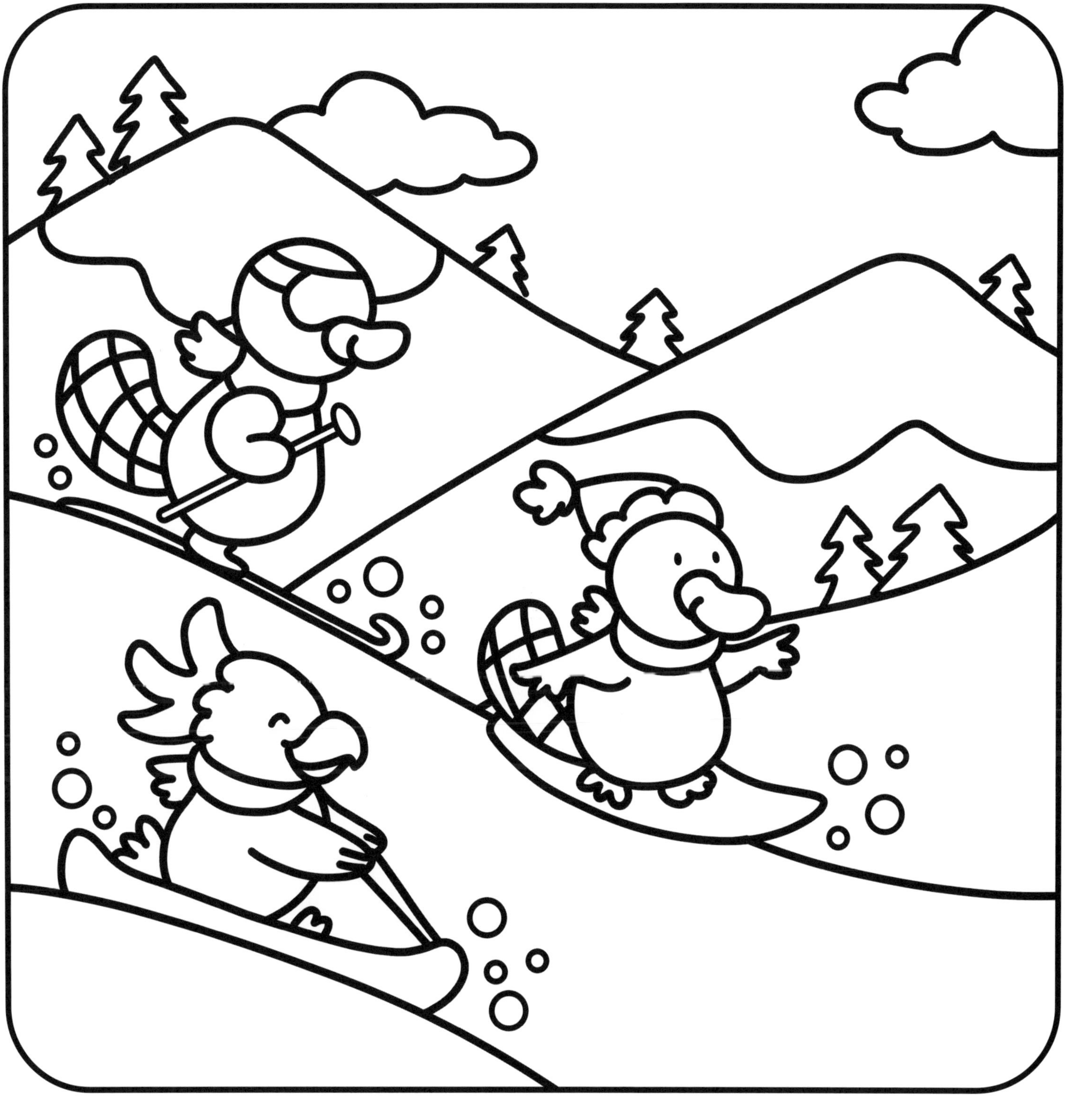

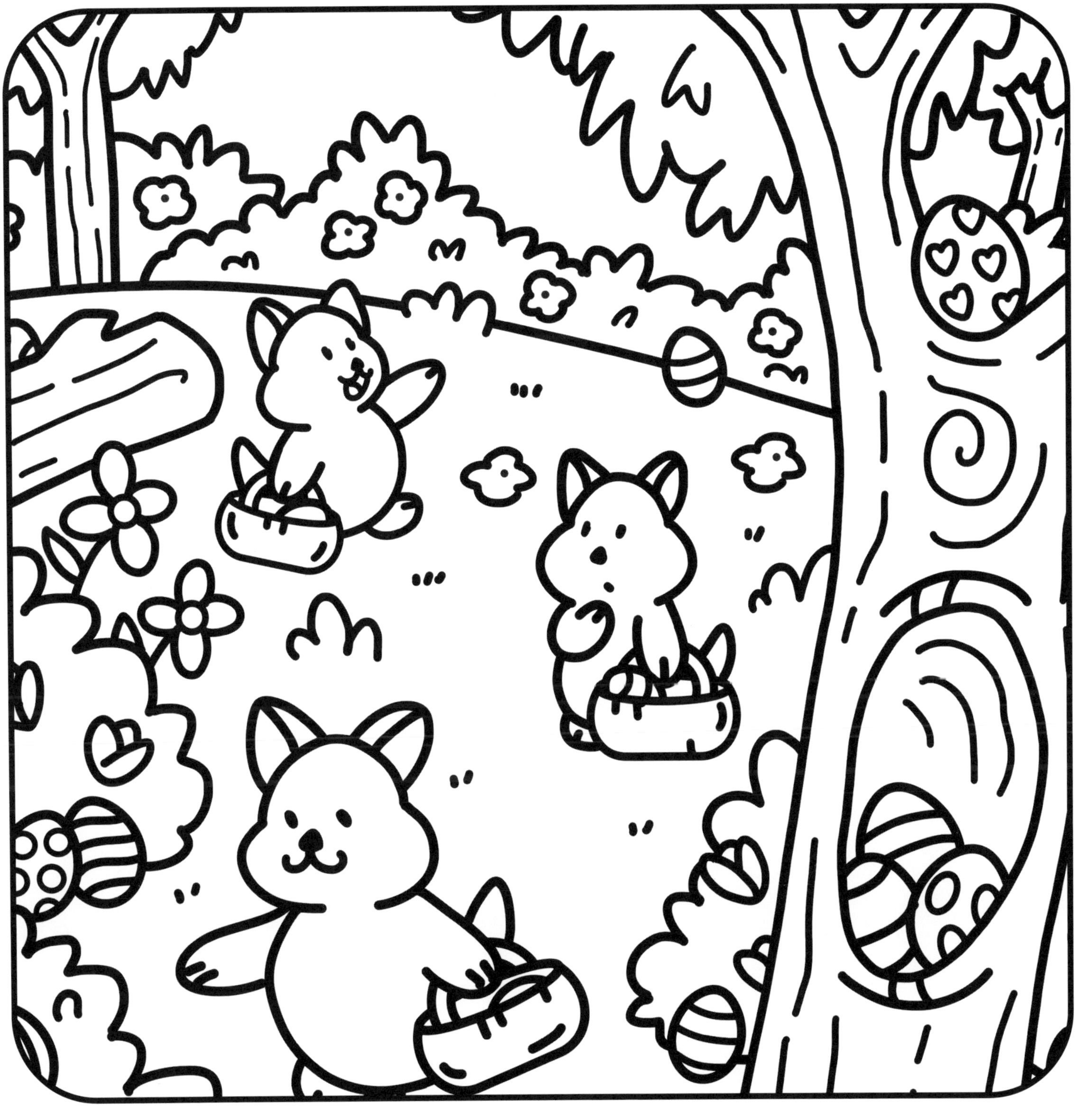

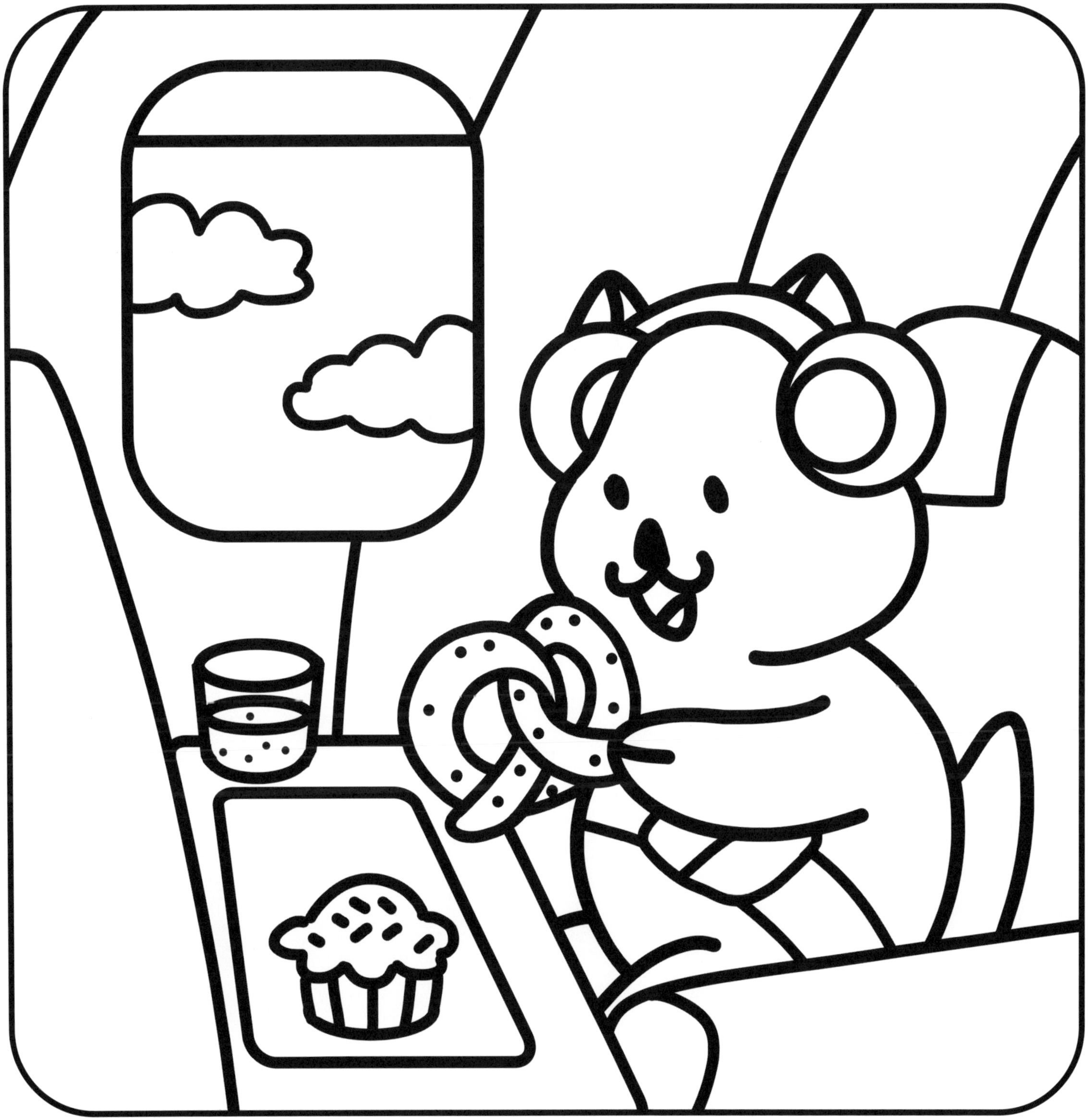

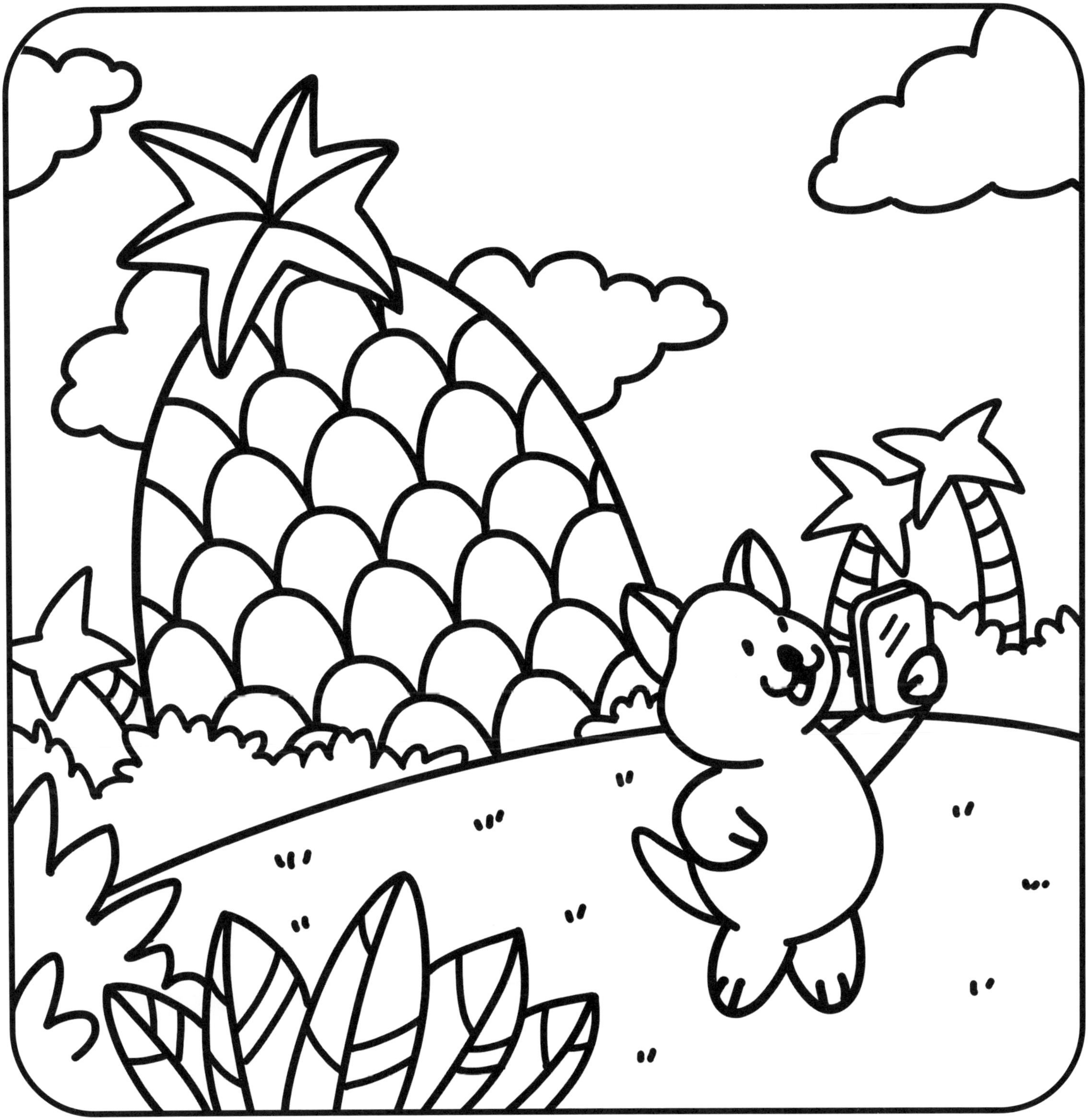

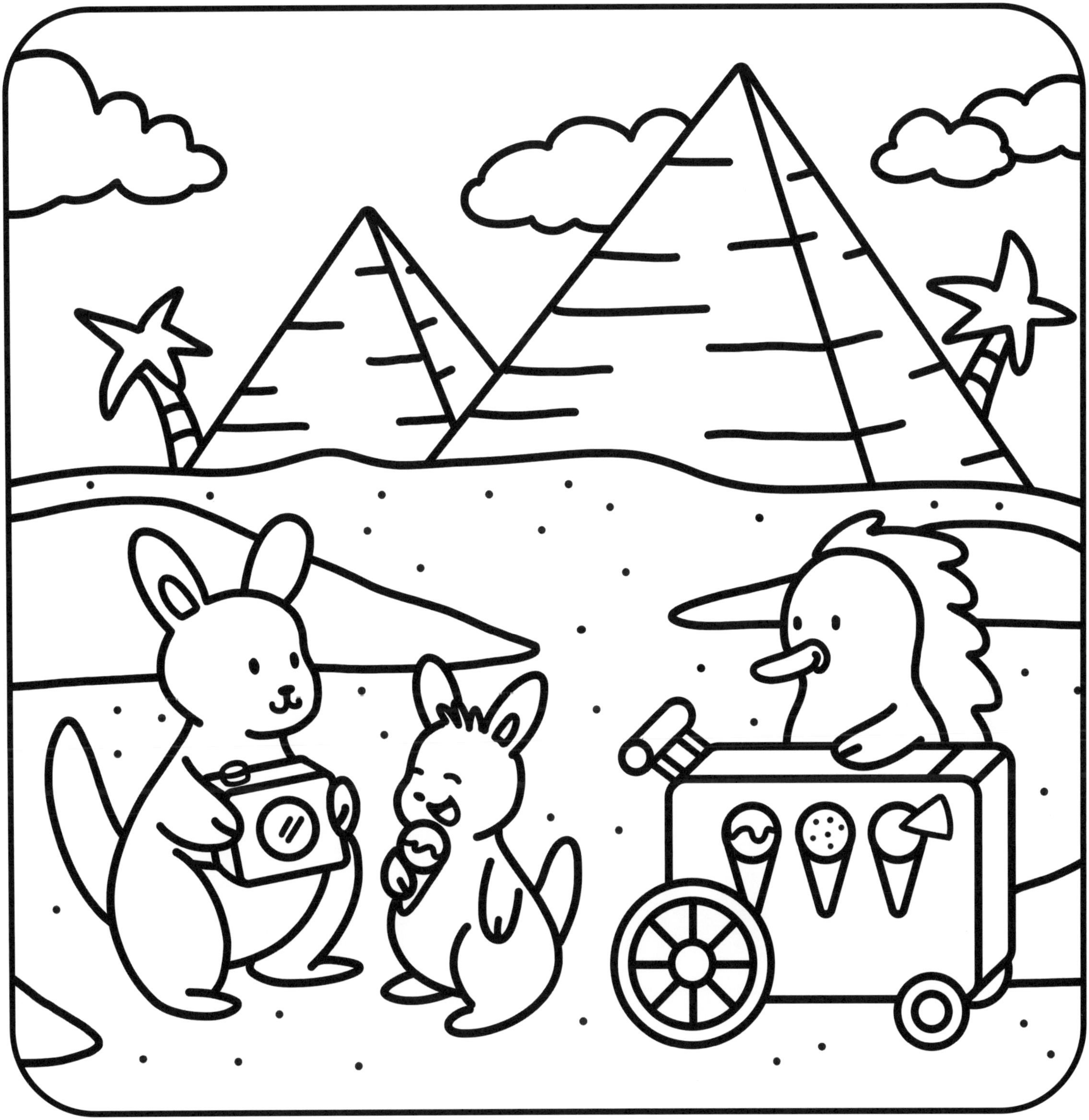

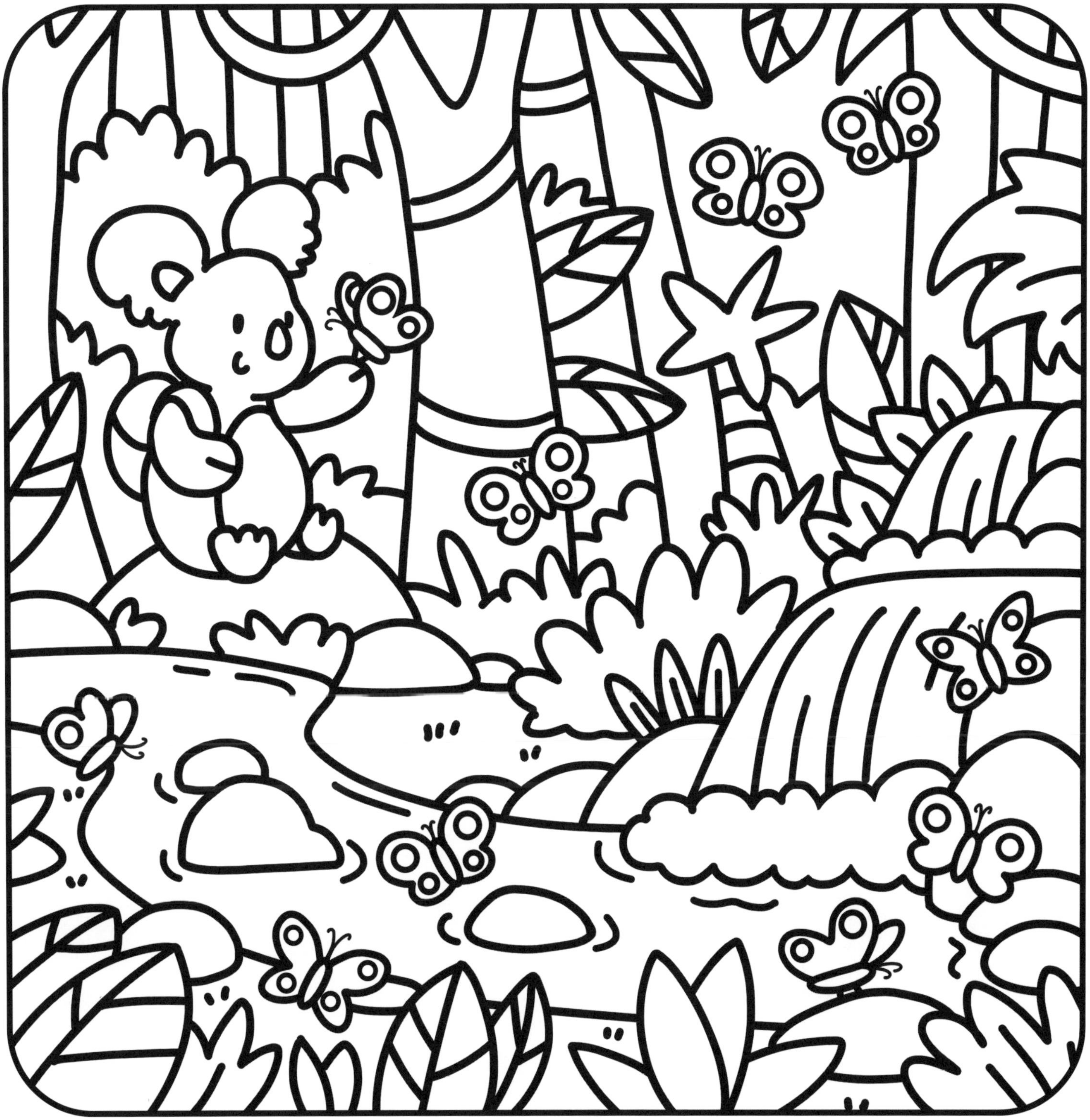

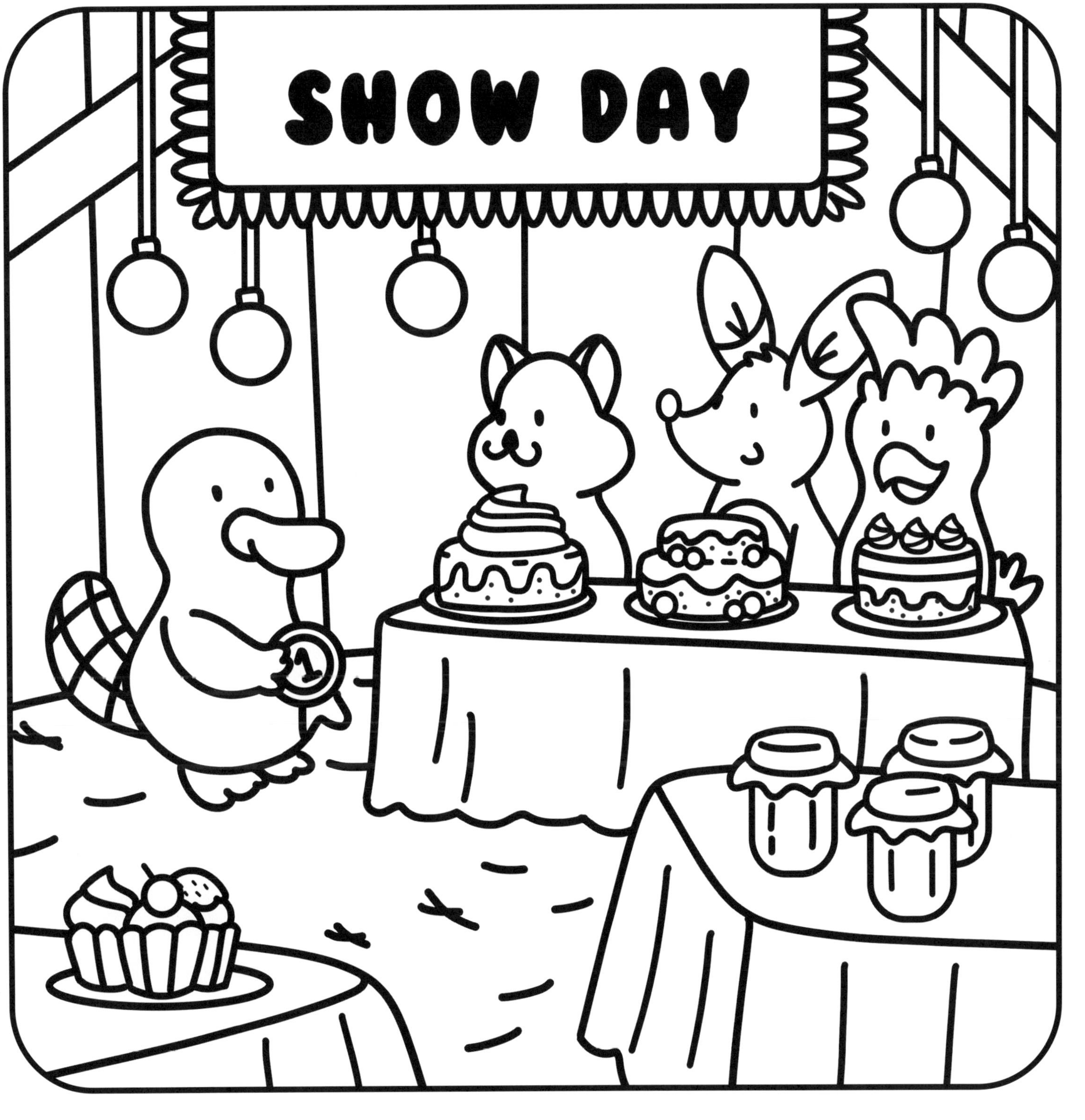
SHOW DAY
1

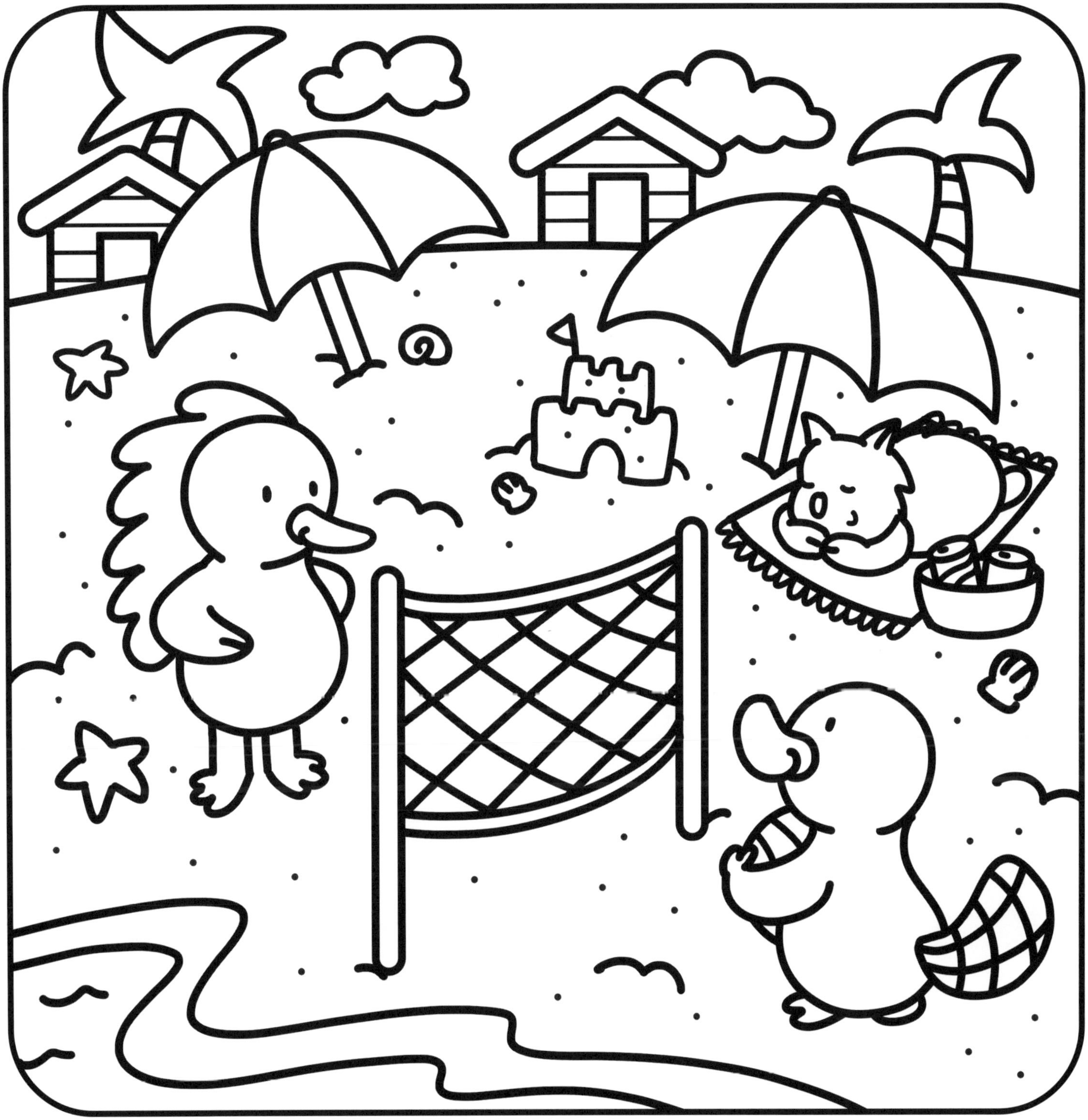

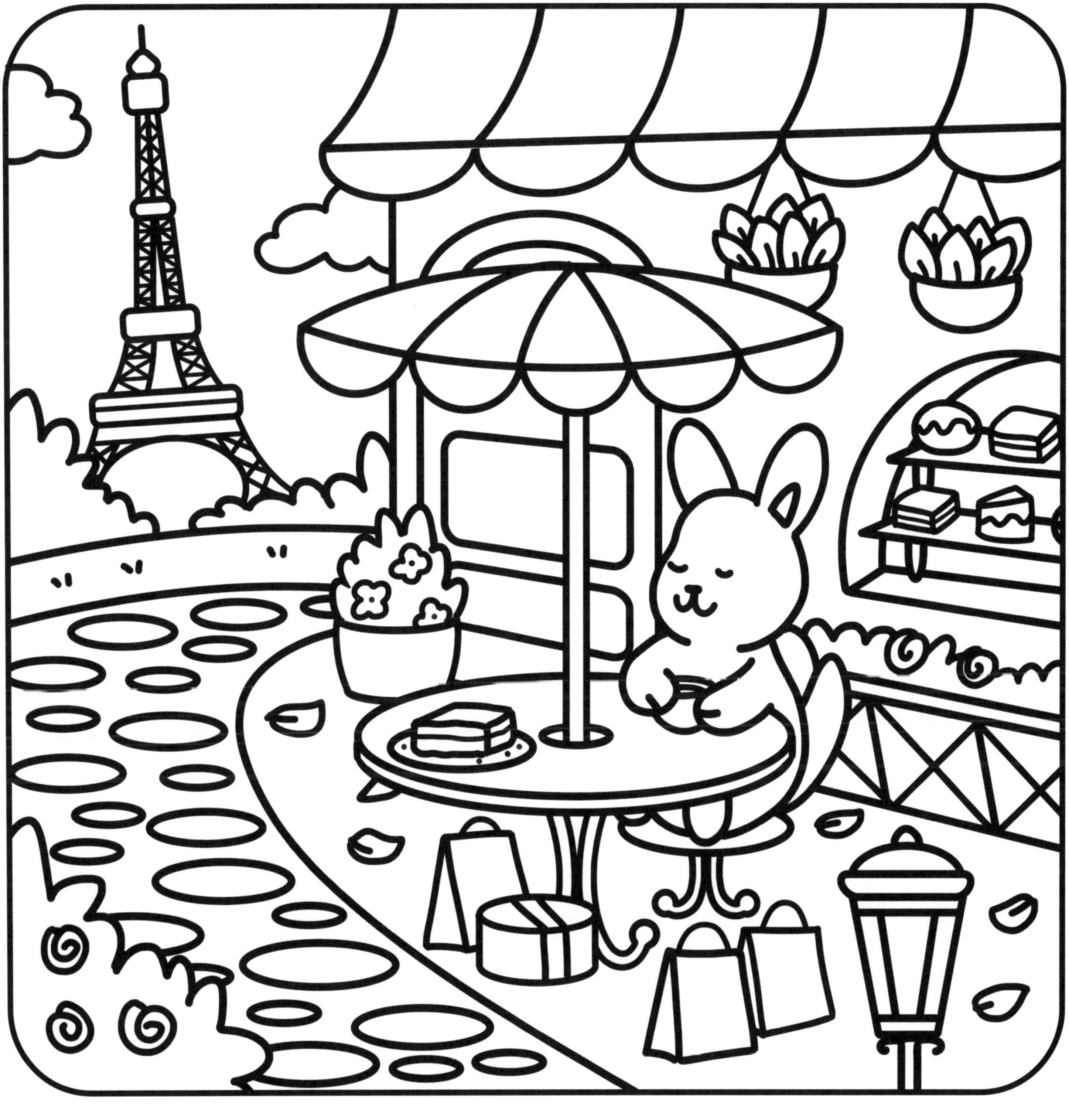

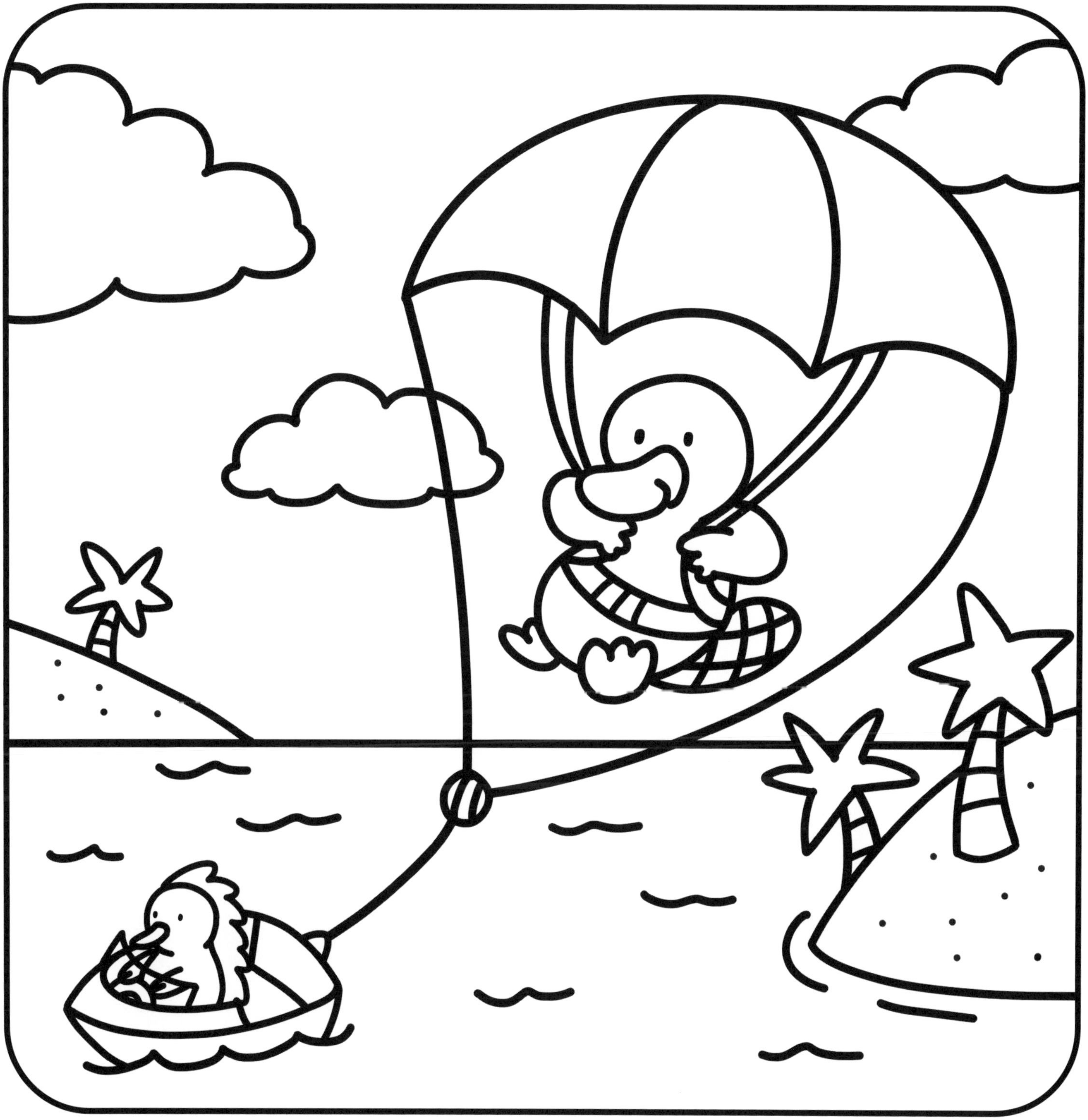

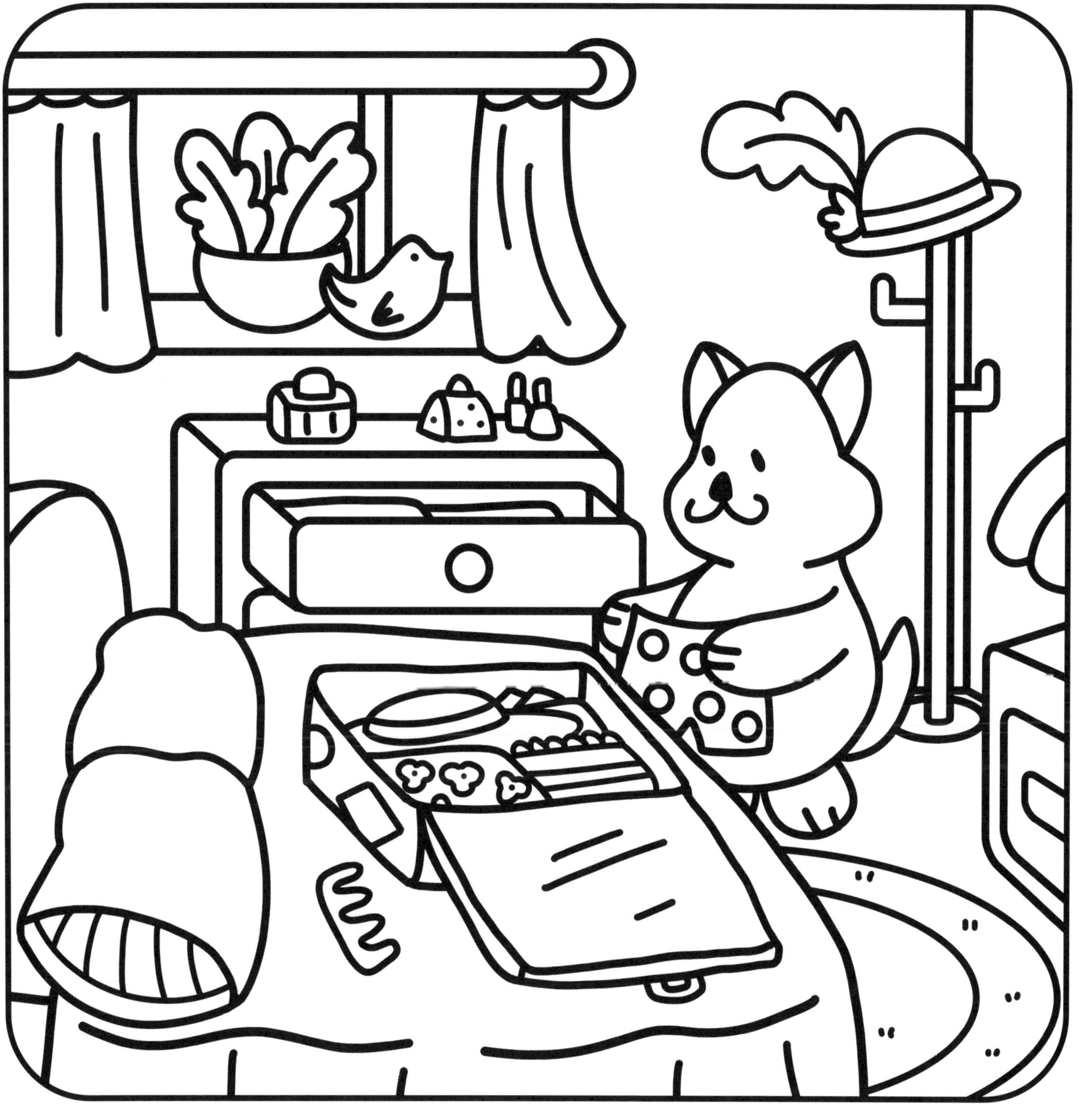

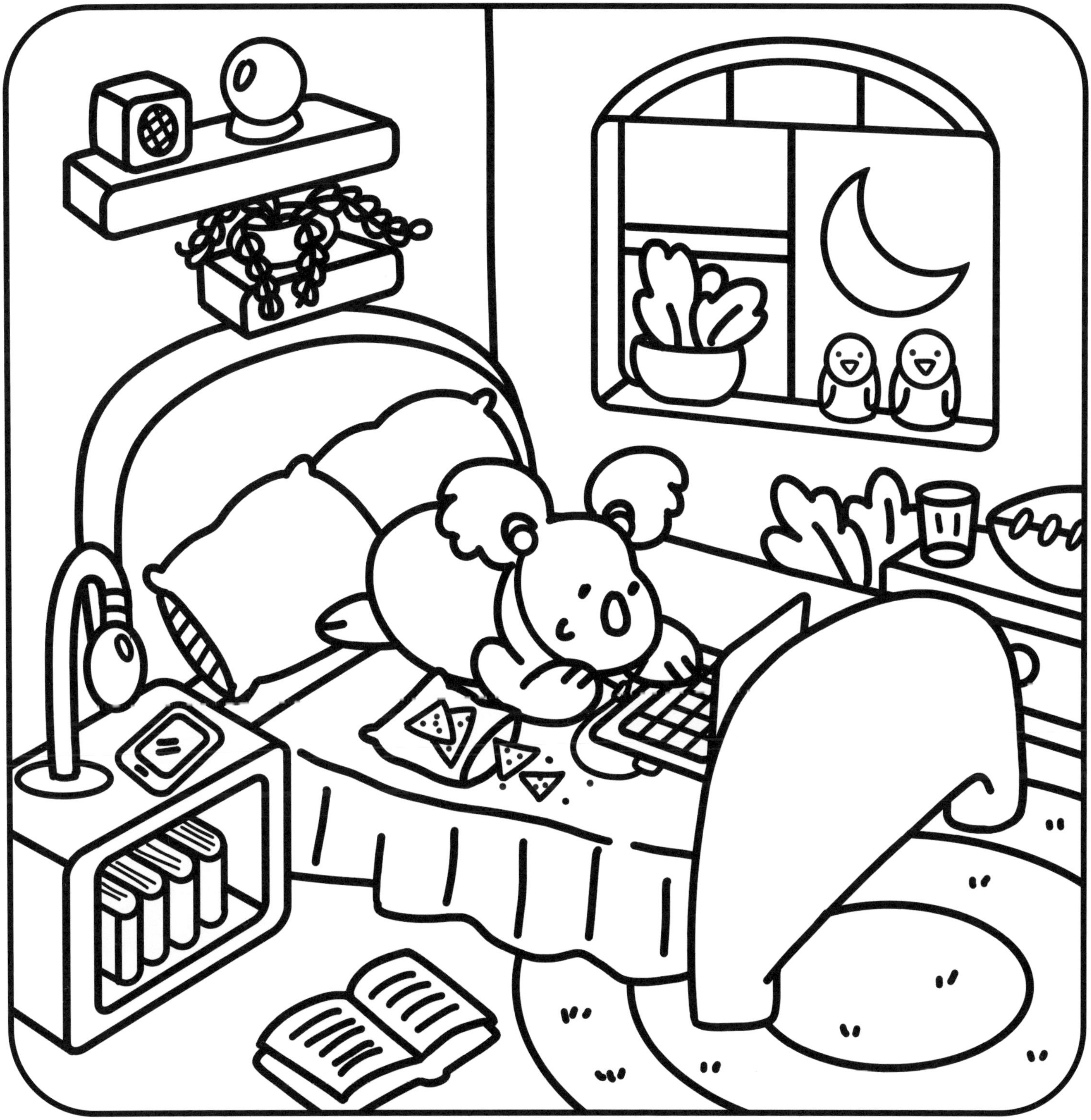

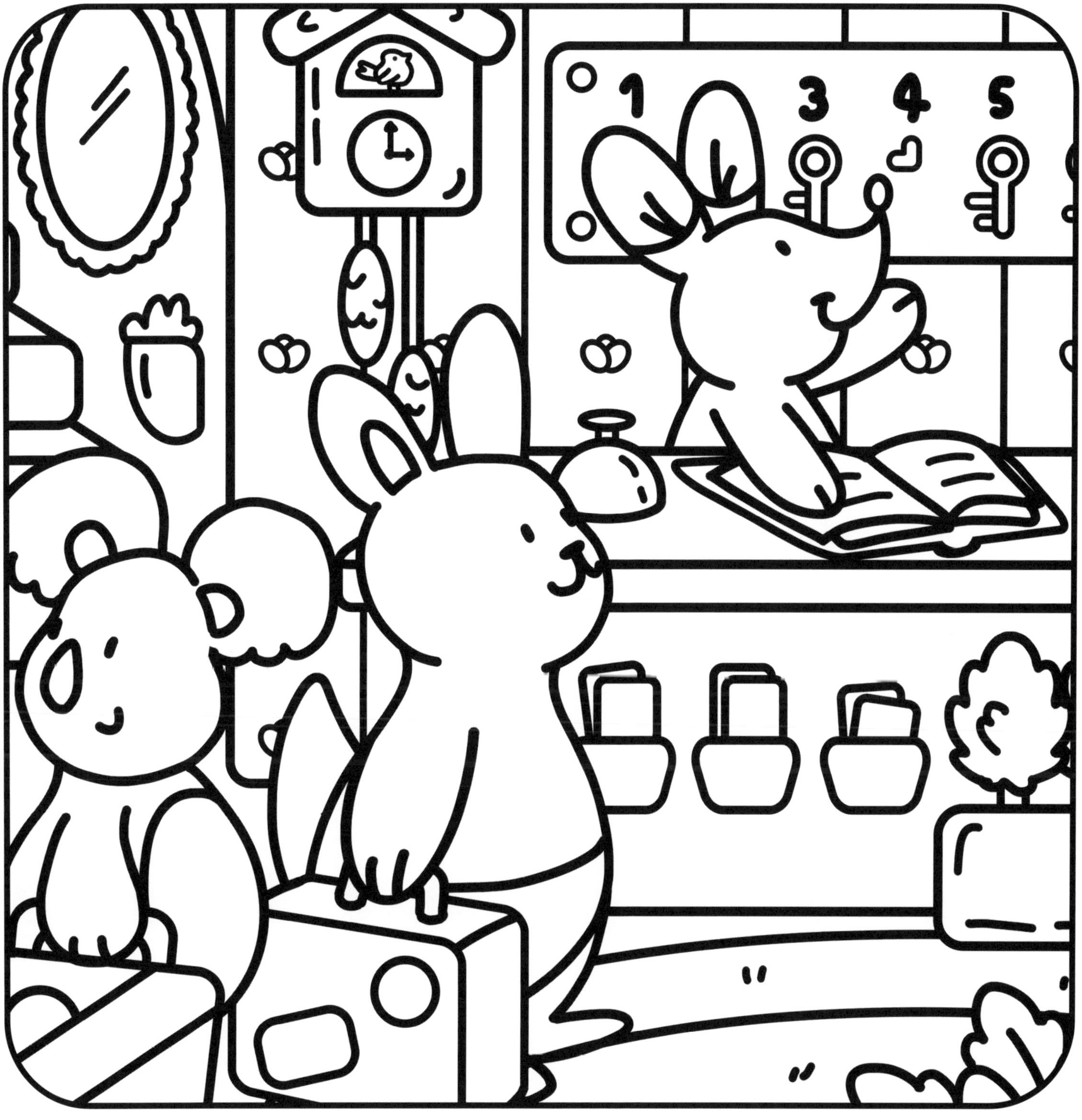
1
3
4
5

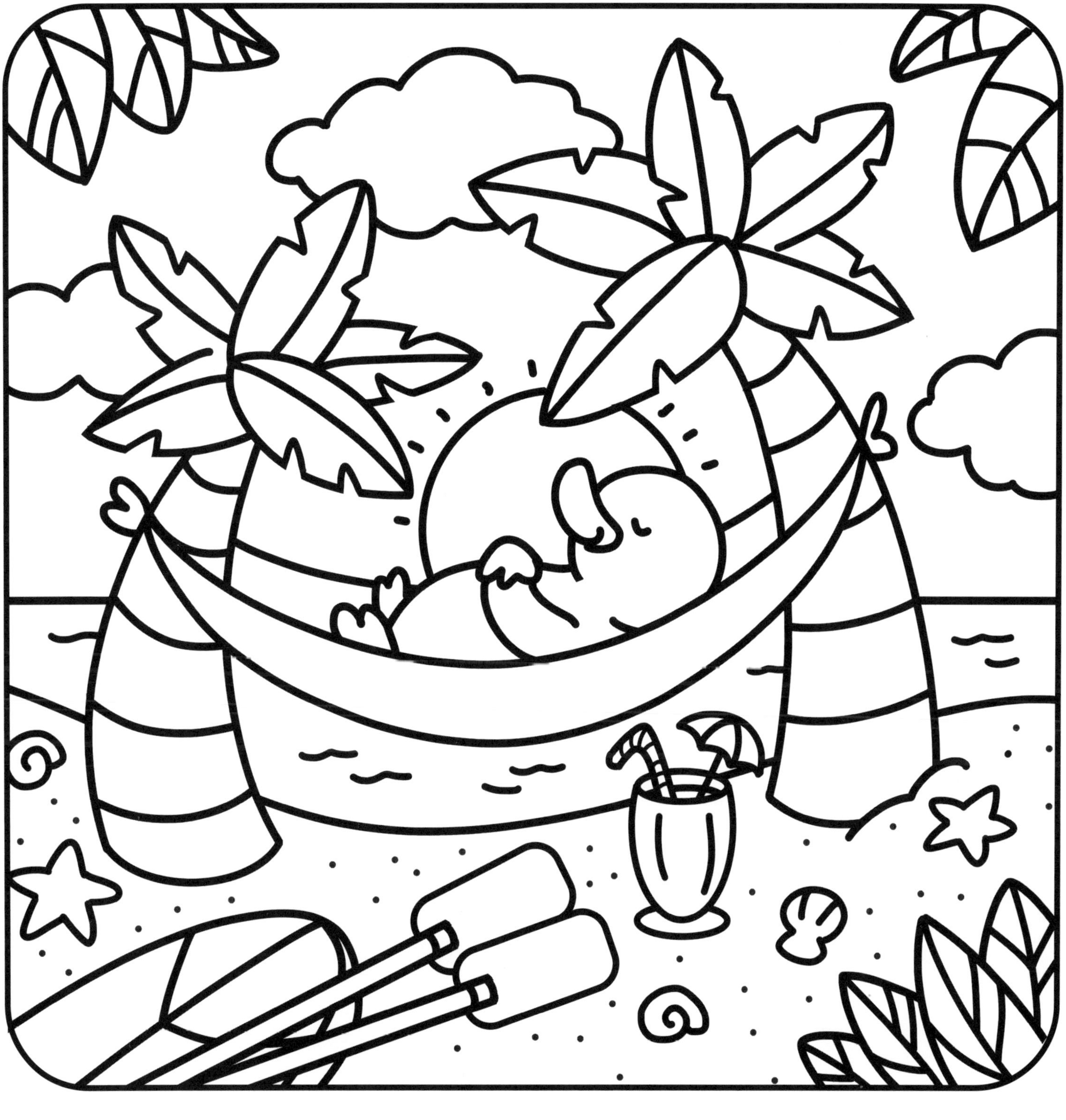

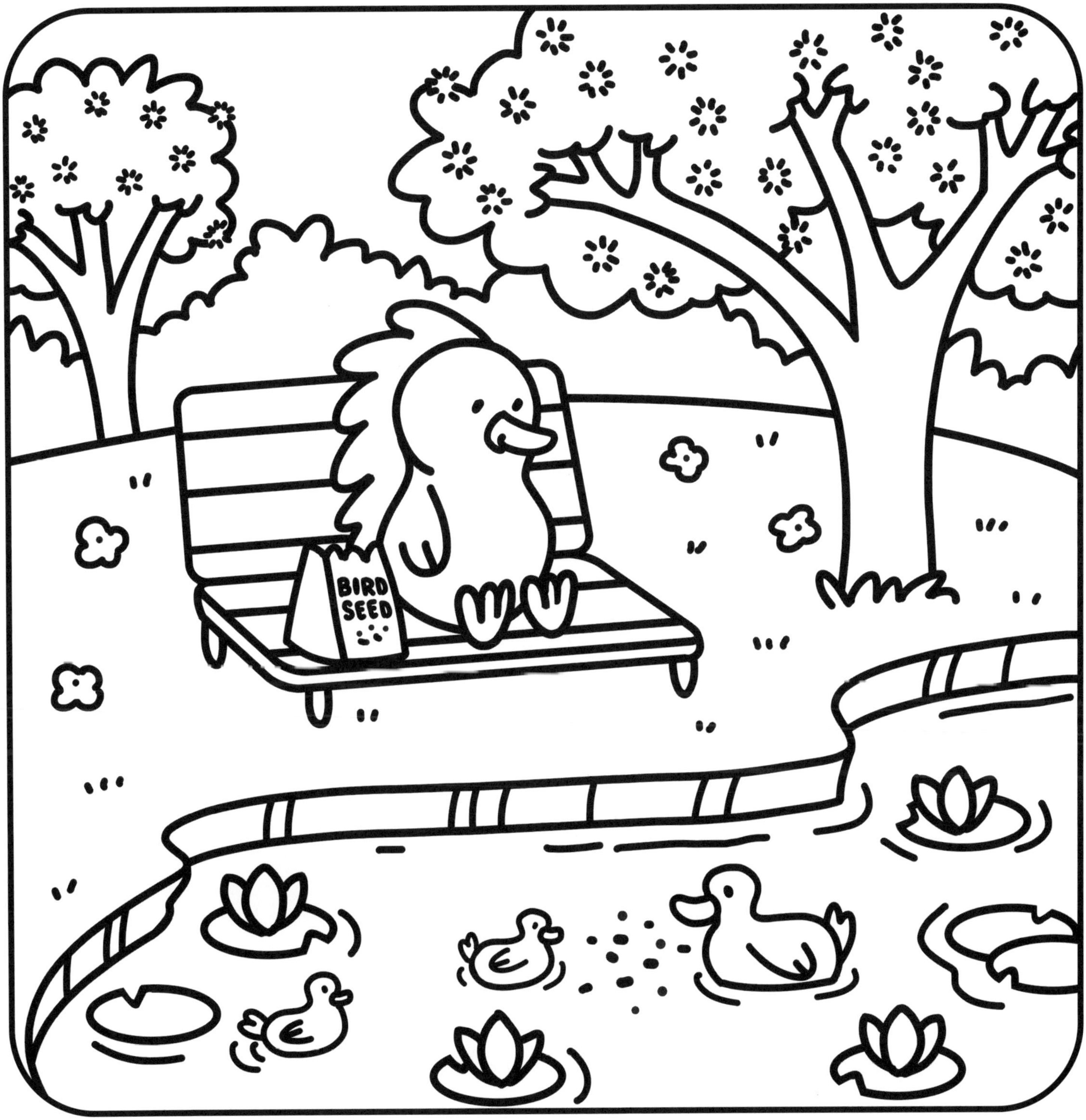
BIRD SEED

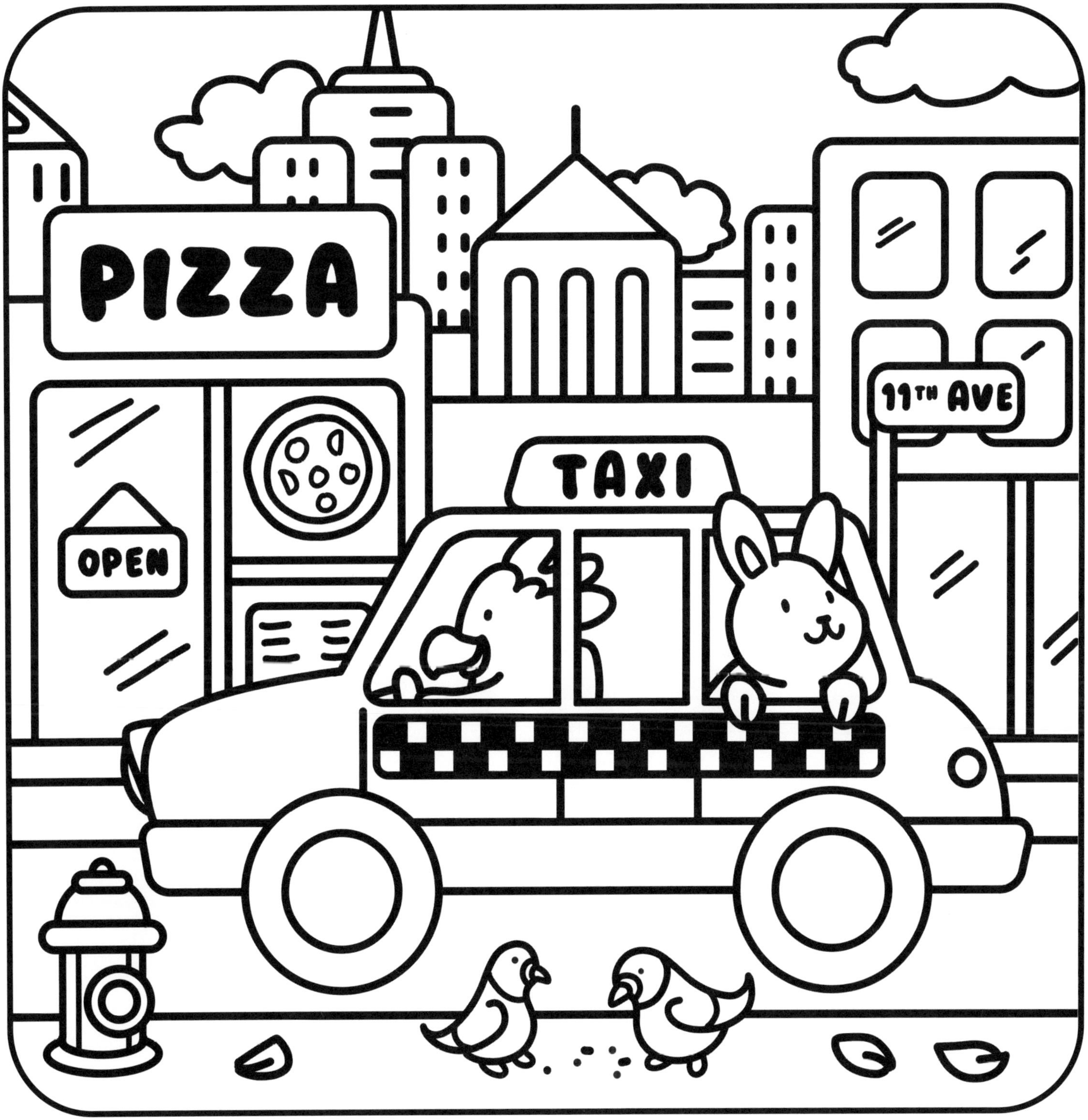
PIZZA
OPEN
TAXI
11TH AVE

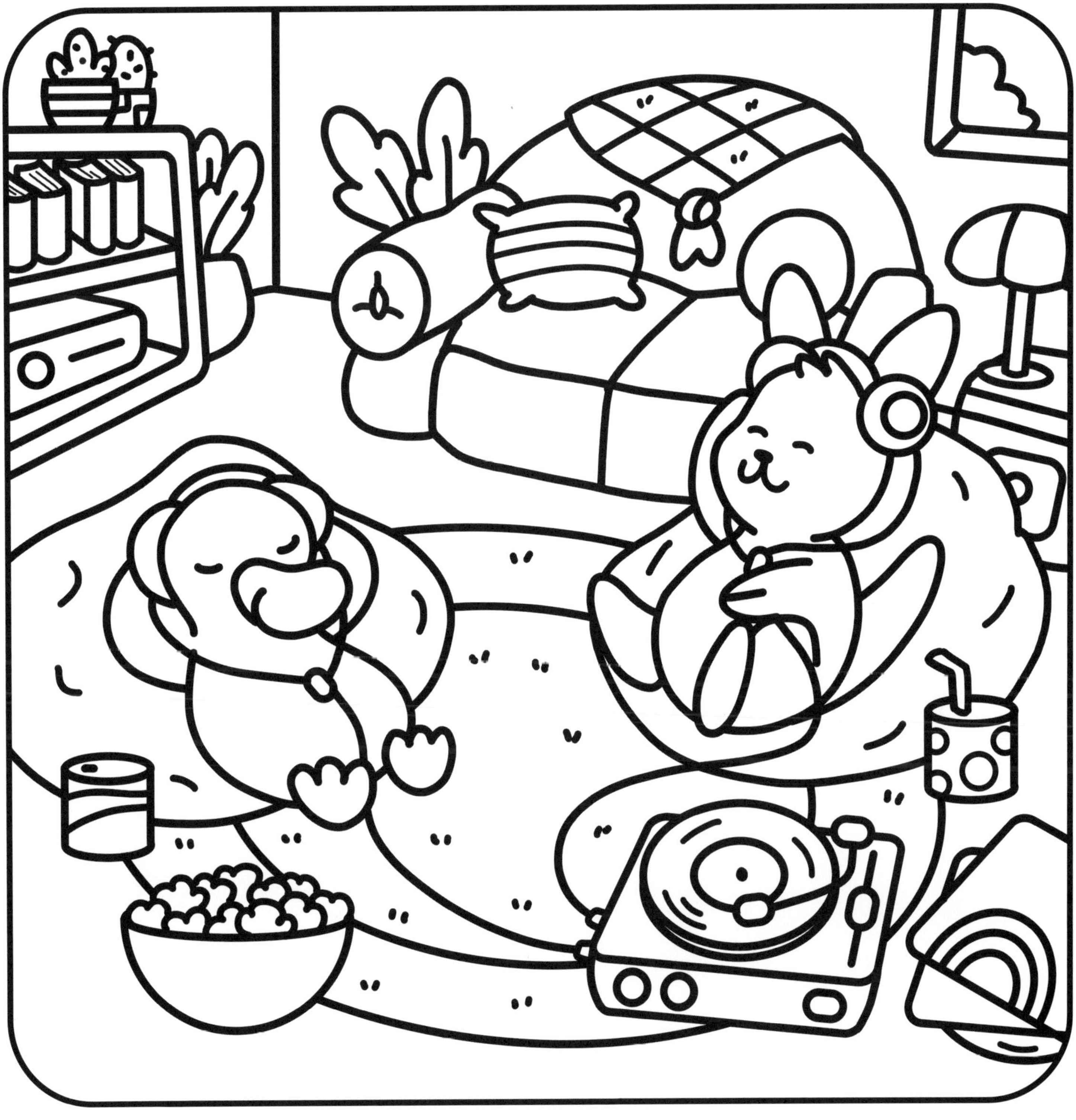

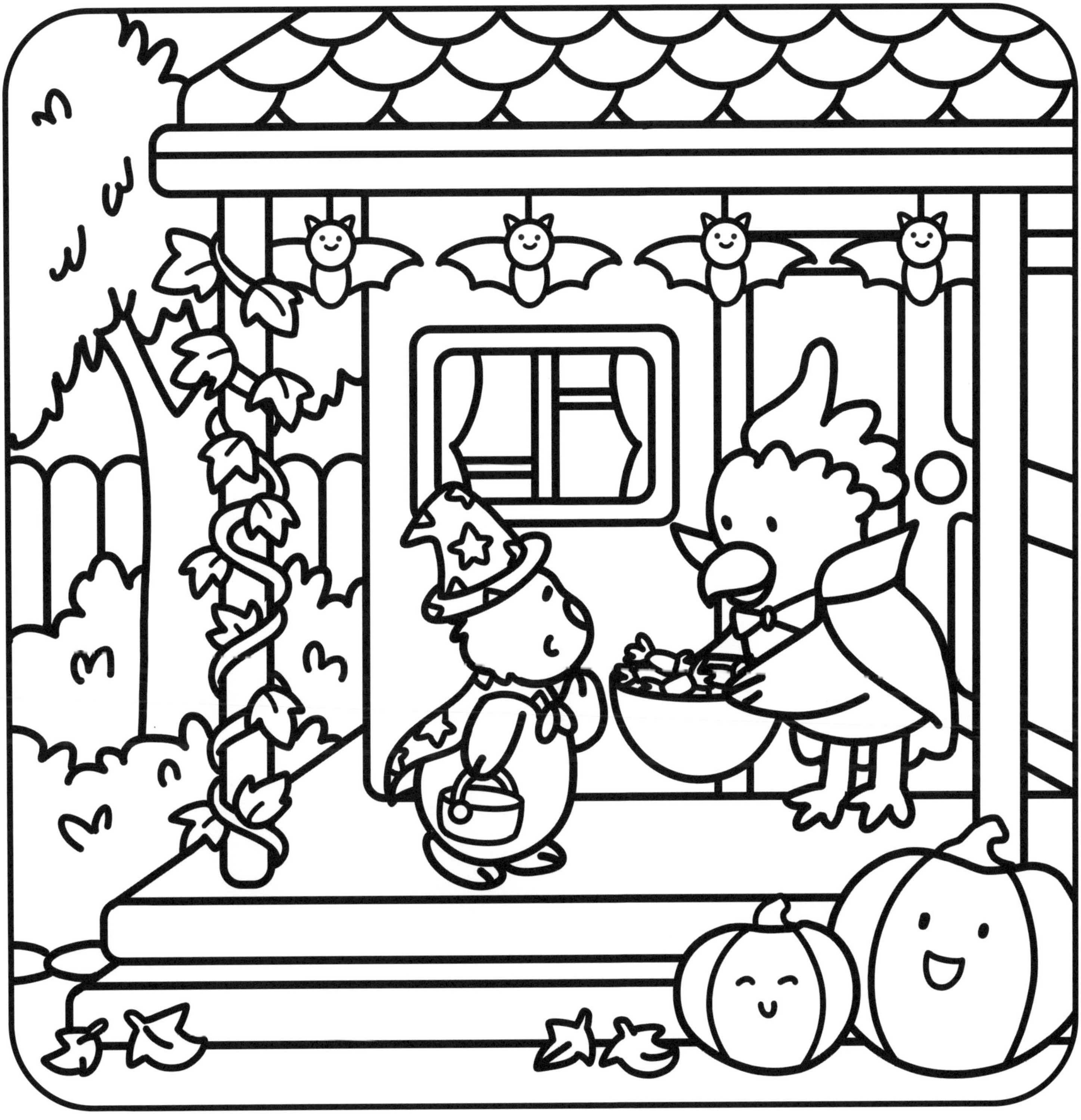

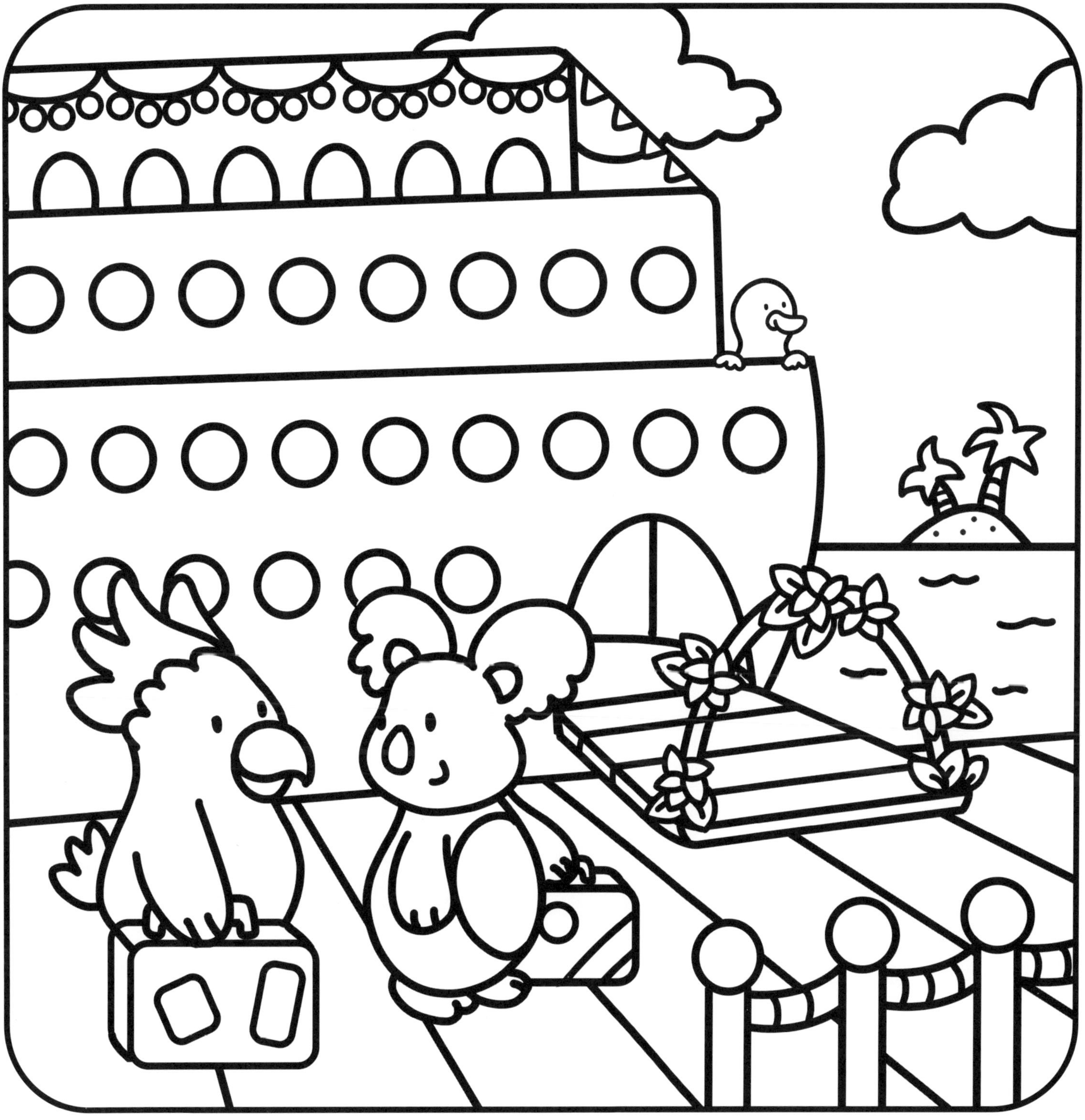

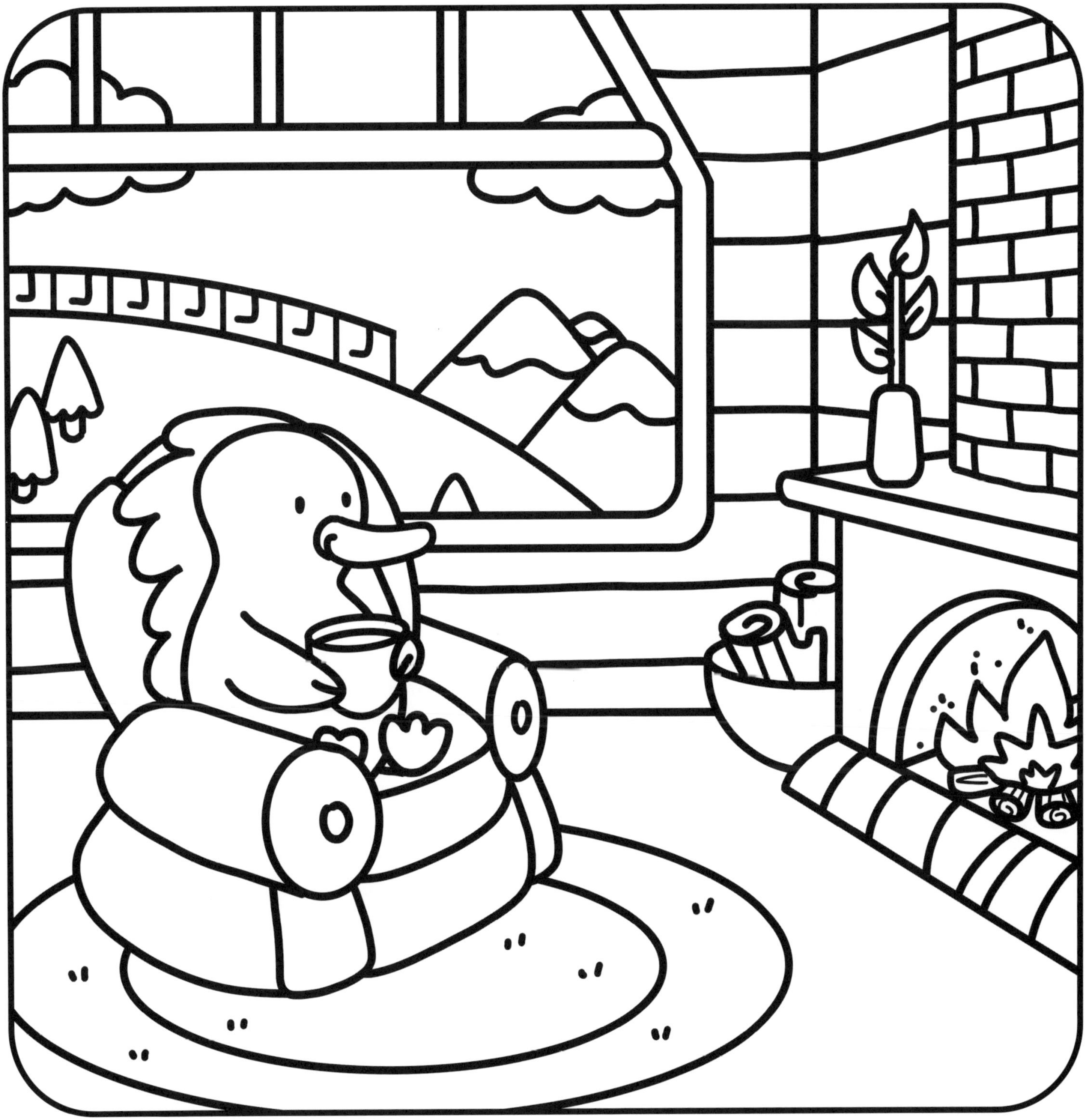

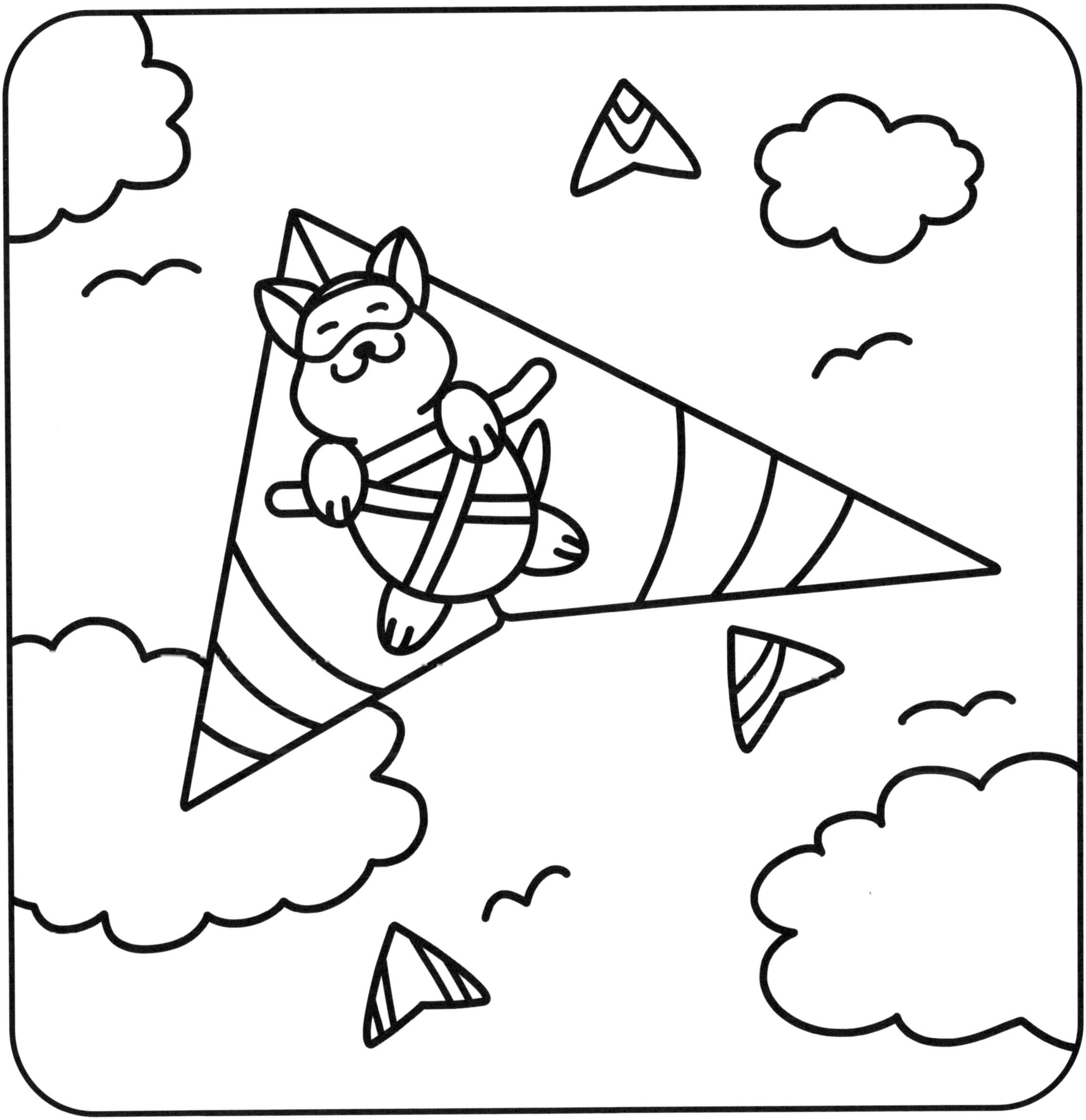

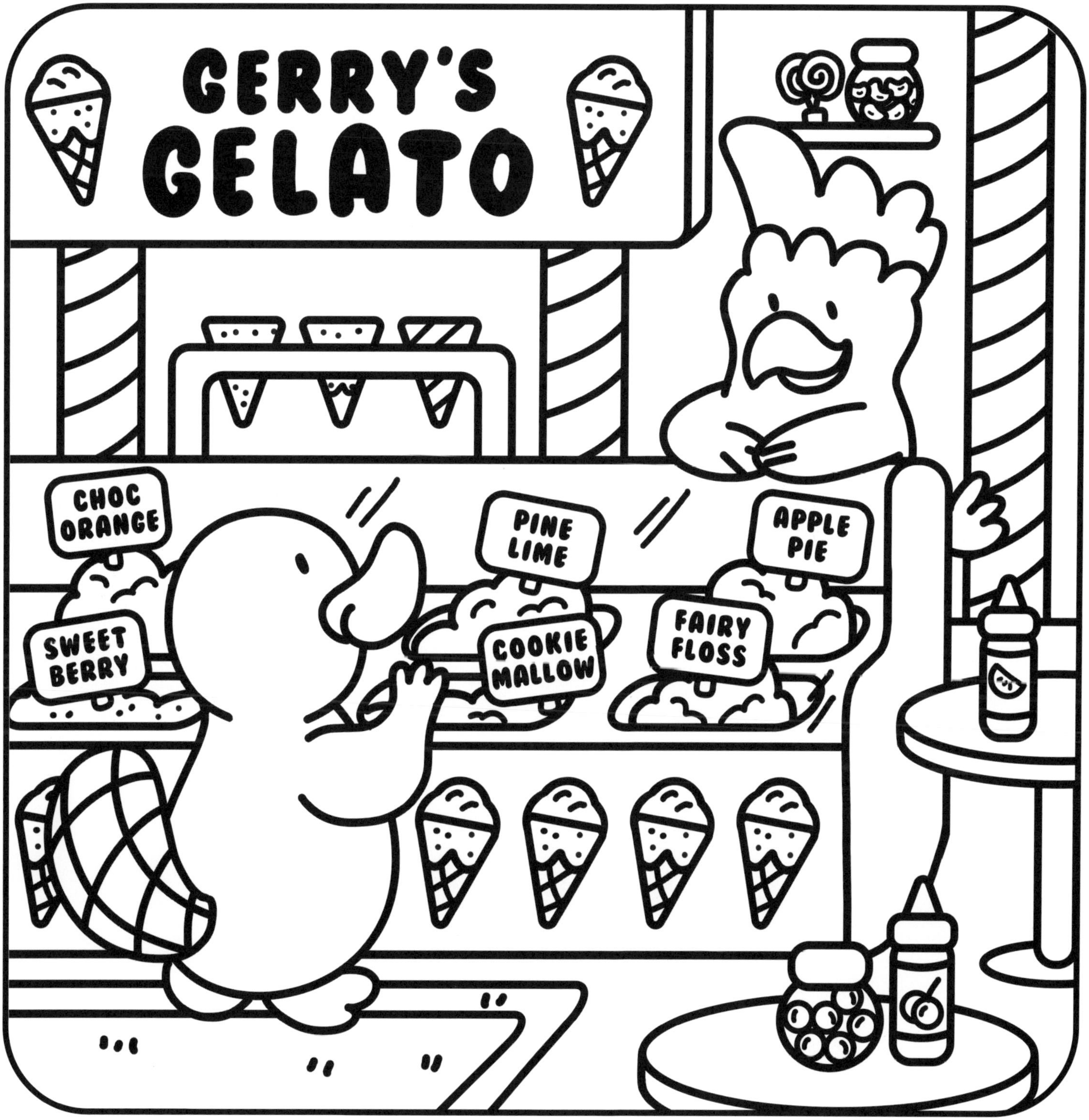
GERRY'S
GELATO
CHOC ORANGE
PINE LIME
APPLE PIE
SWEET BERRY
COOKIE MALLOW
FAIRY FLOSS

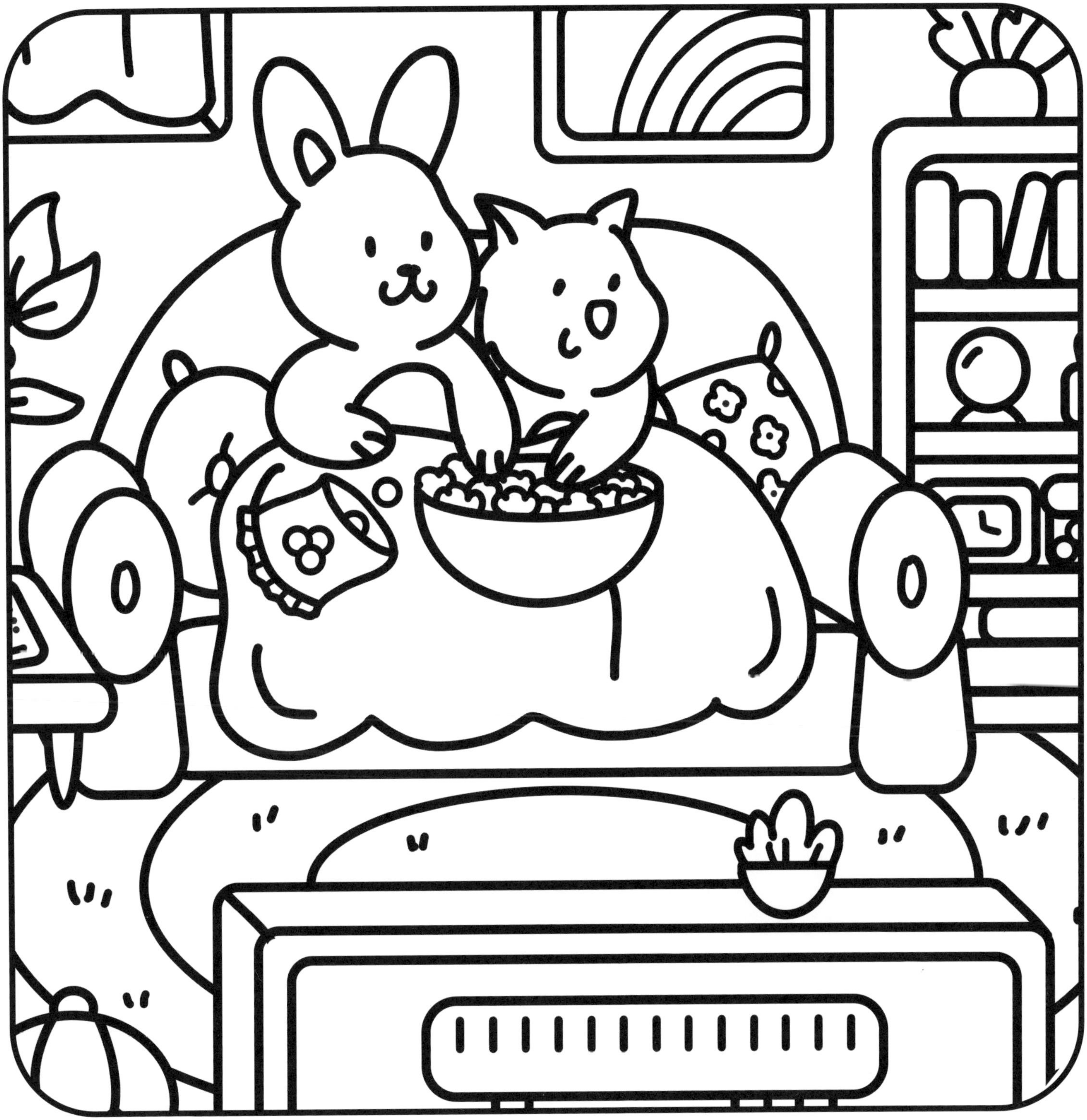

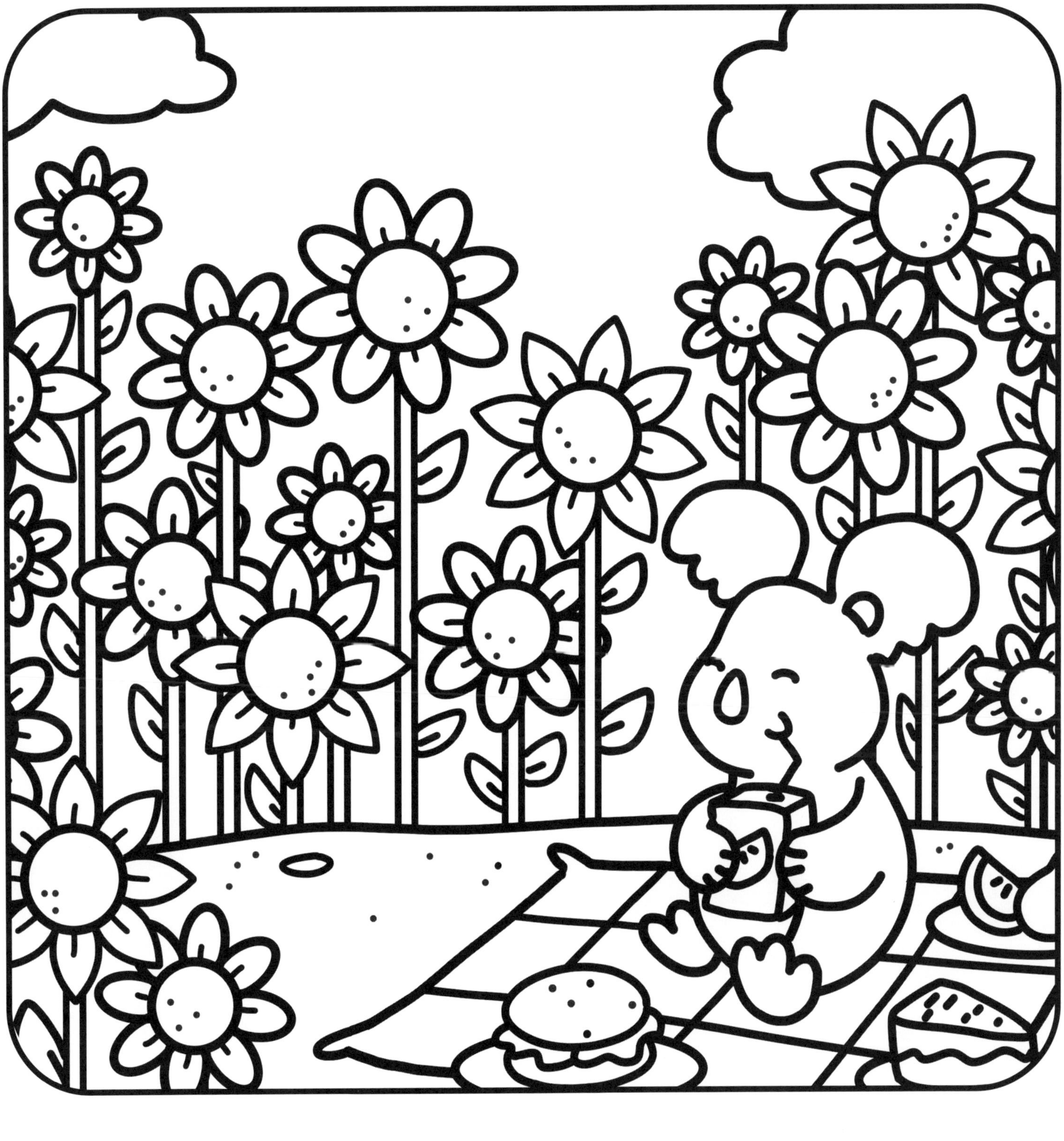

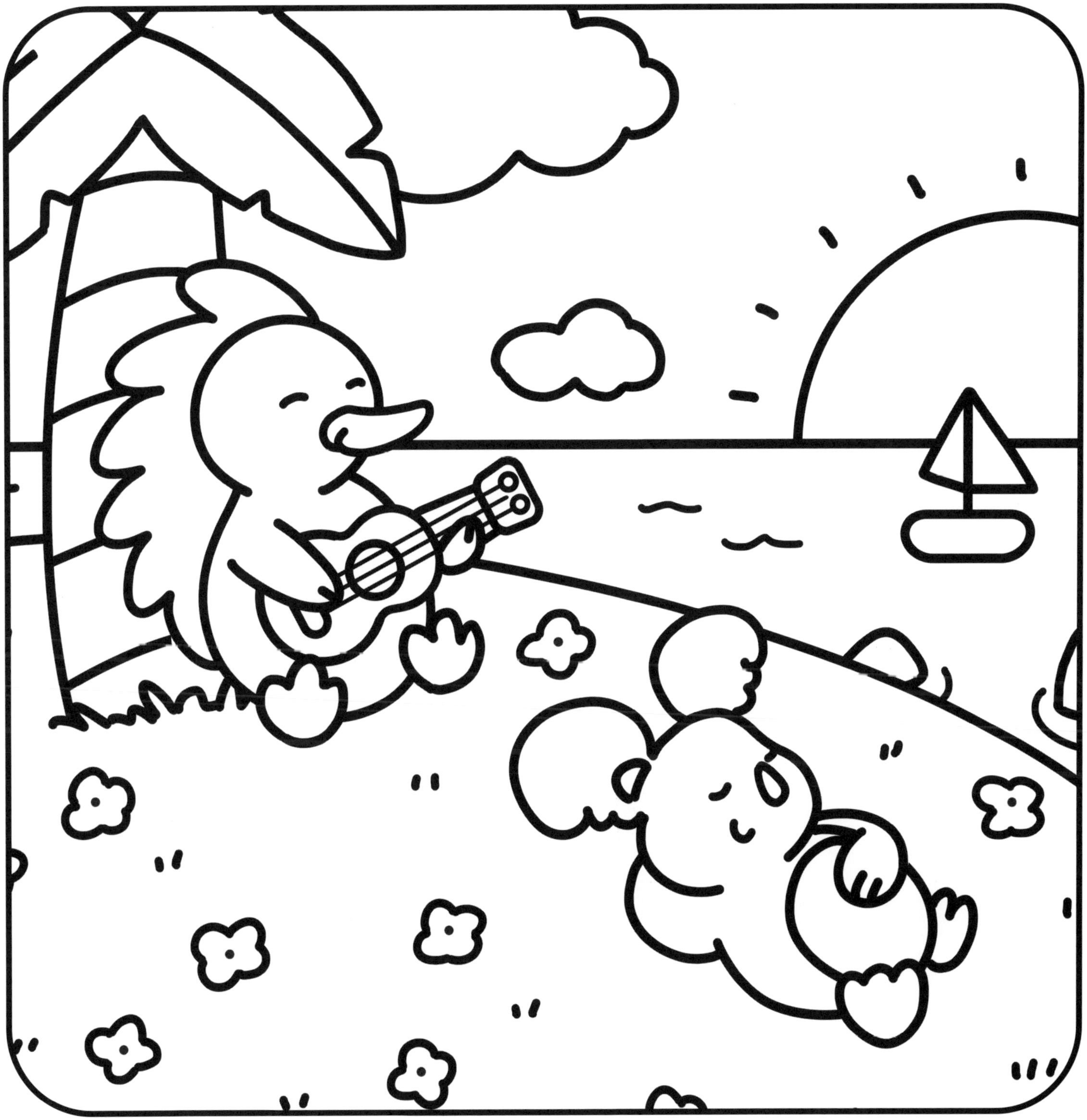

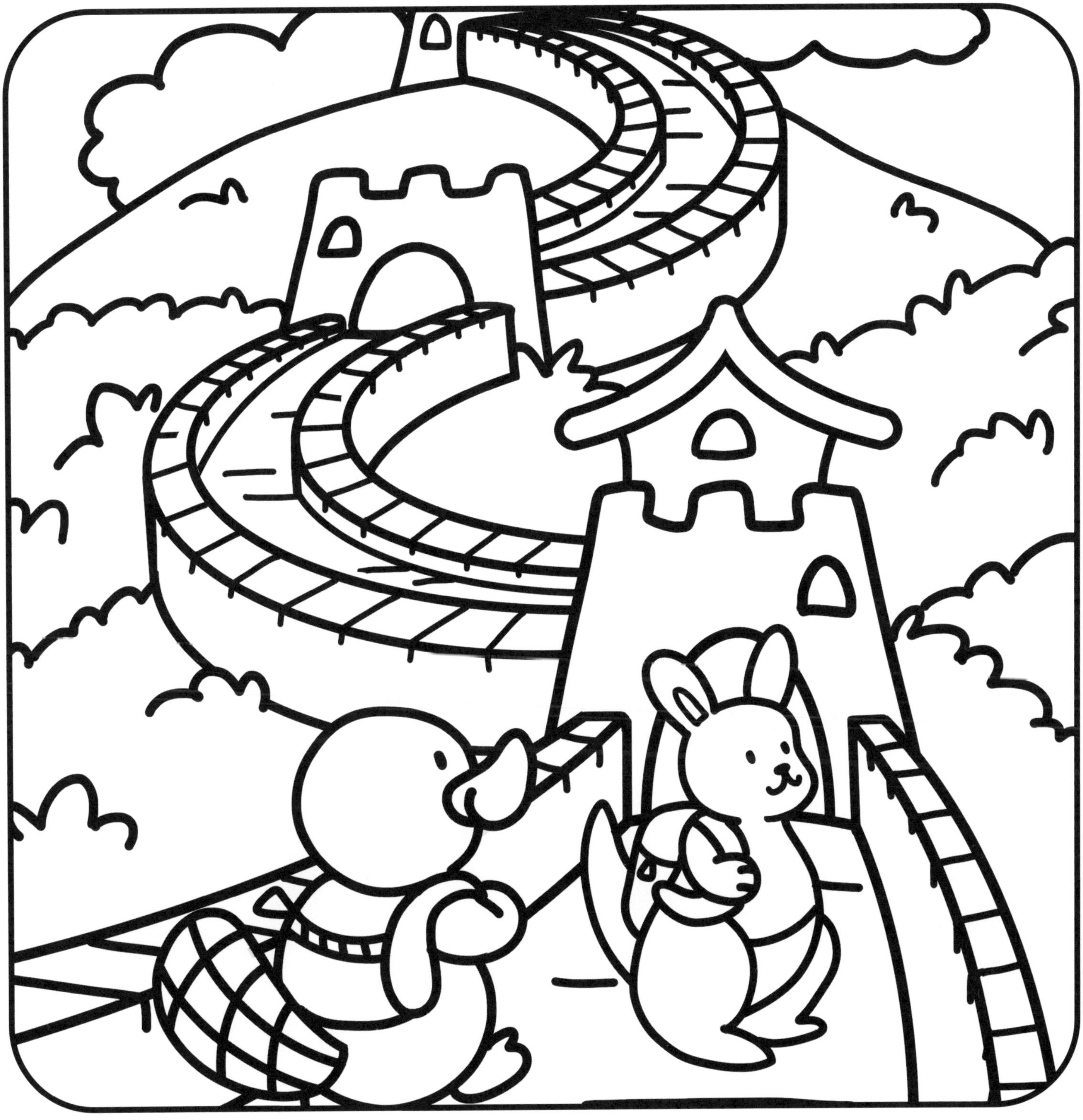

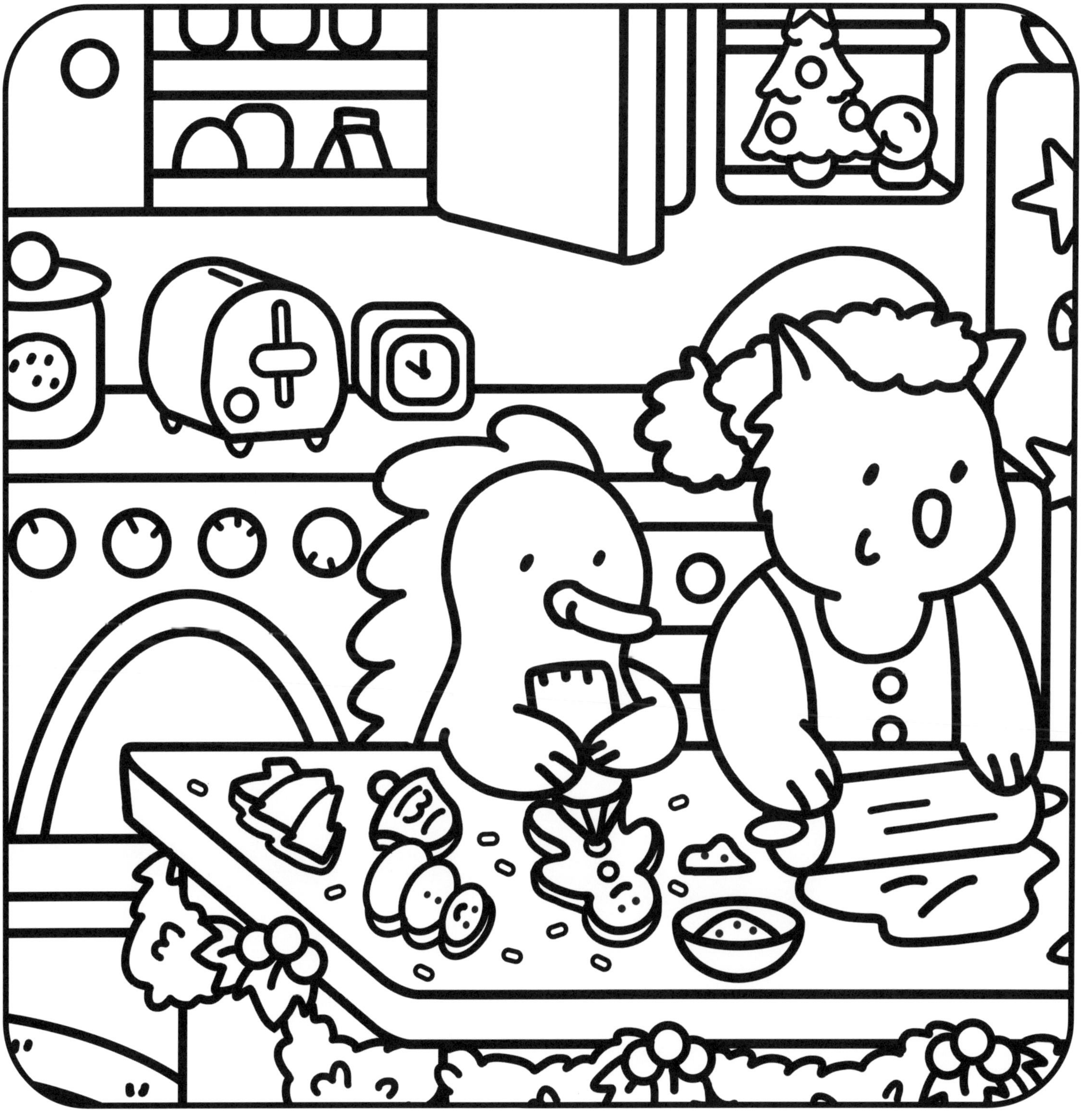

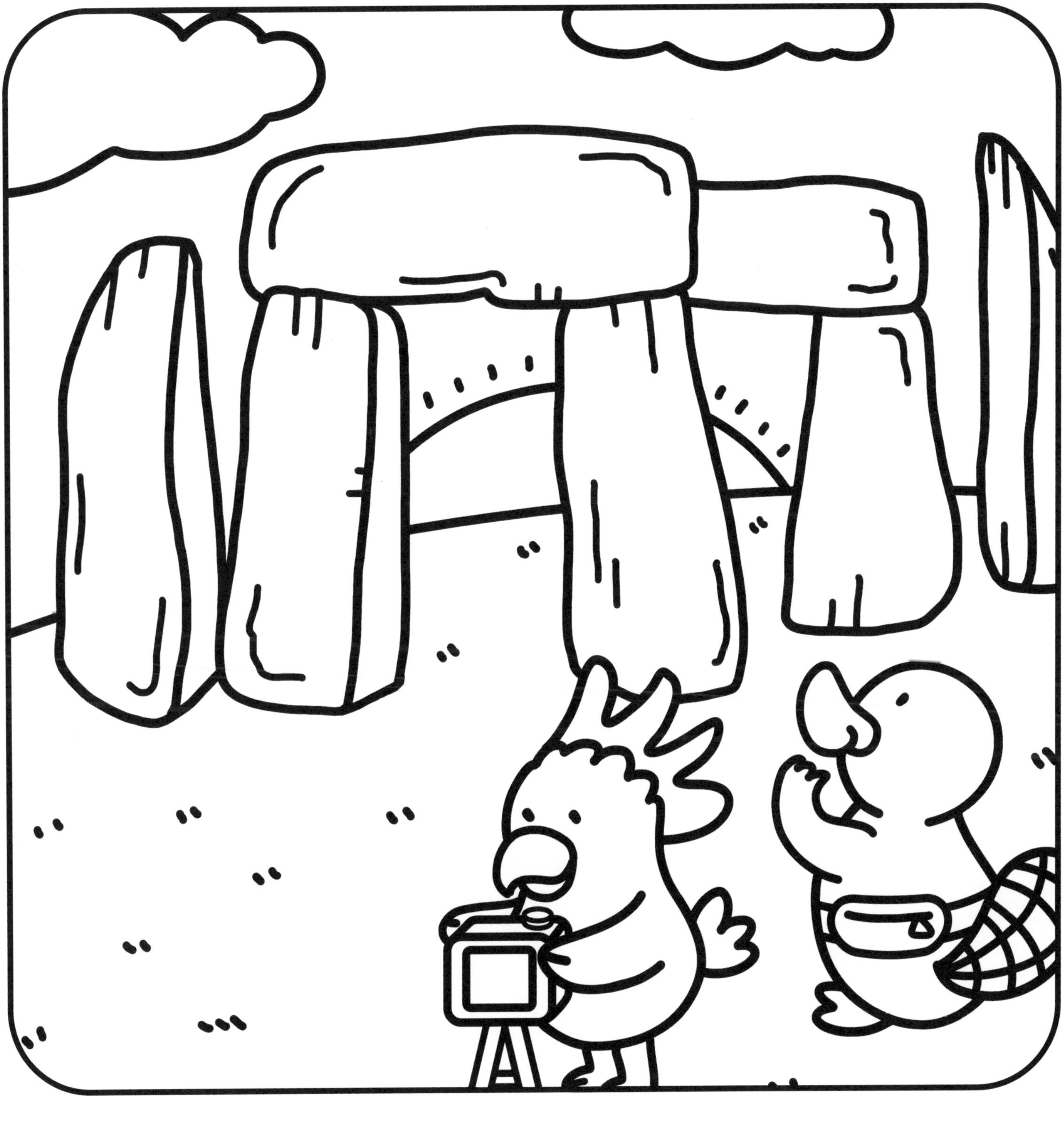

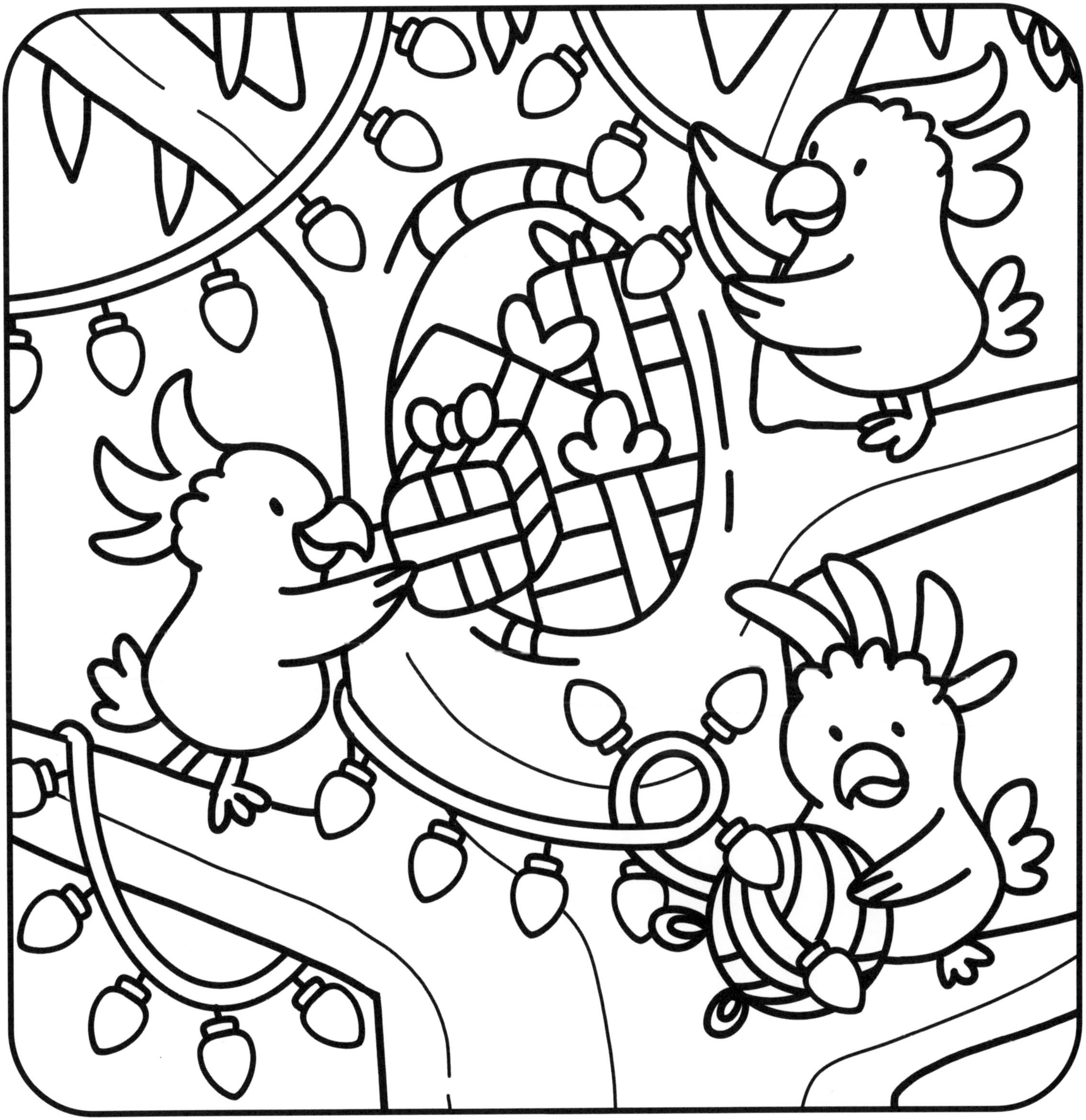

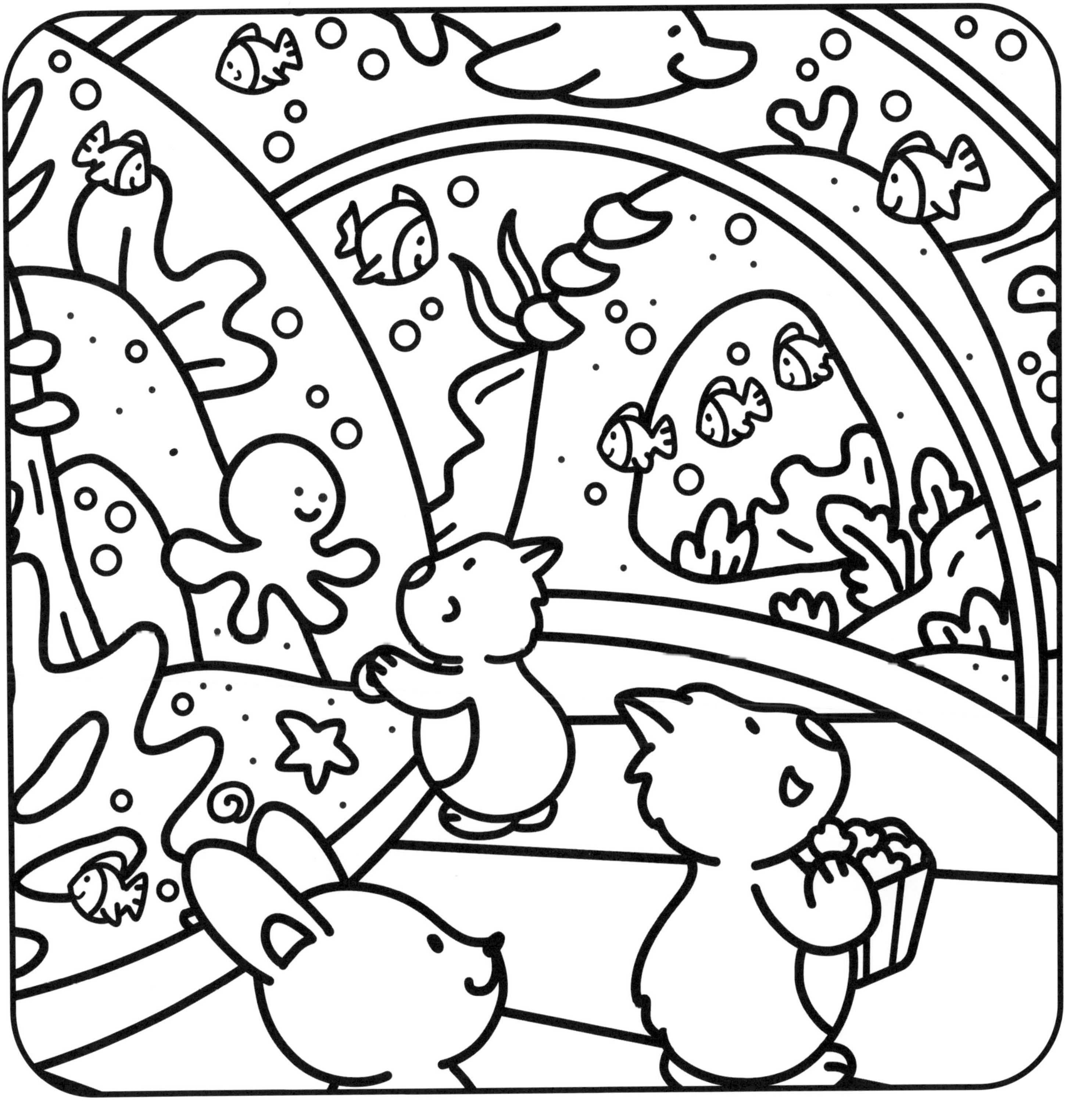

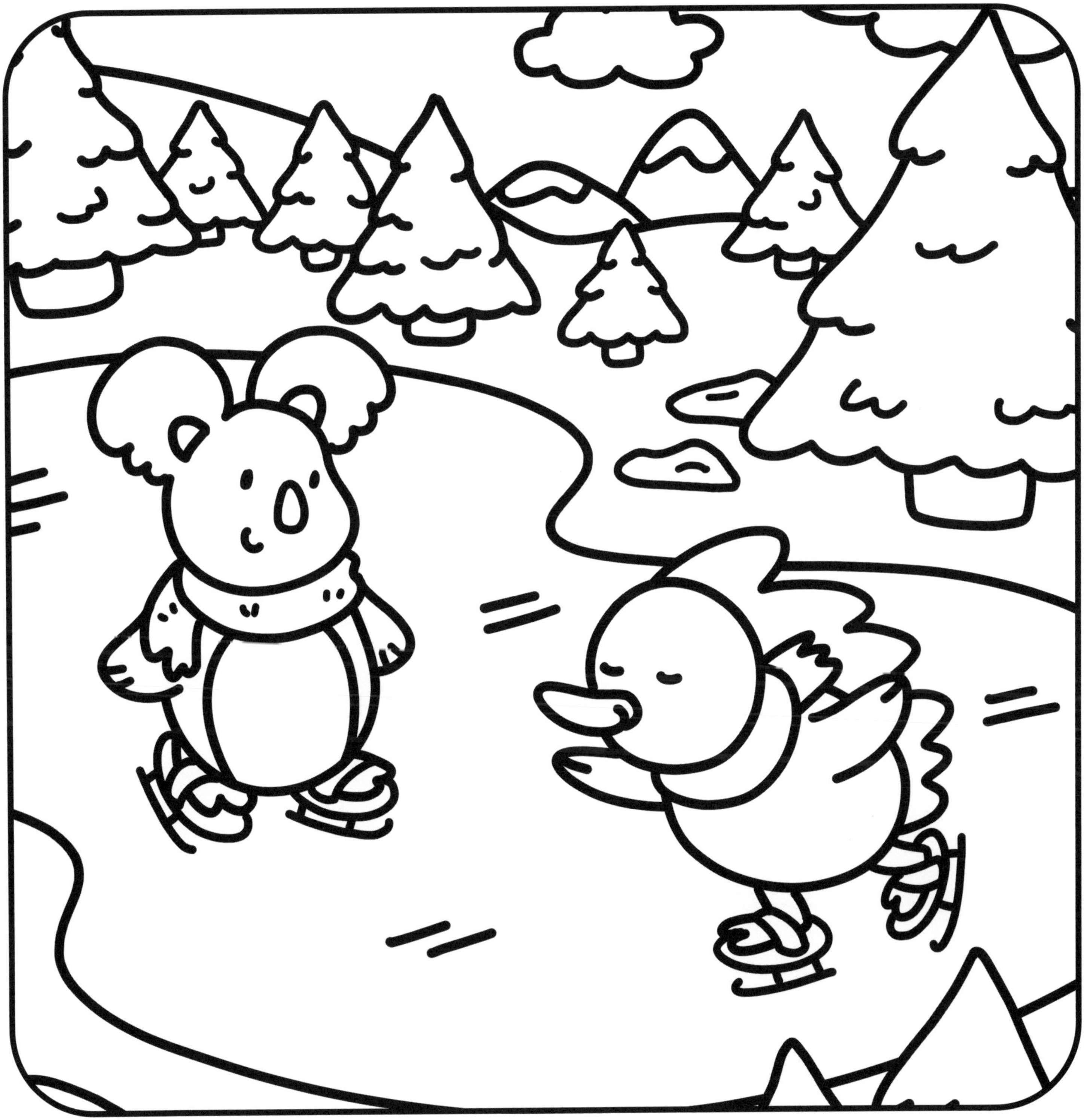

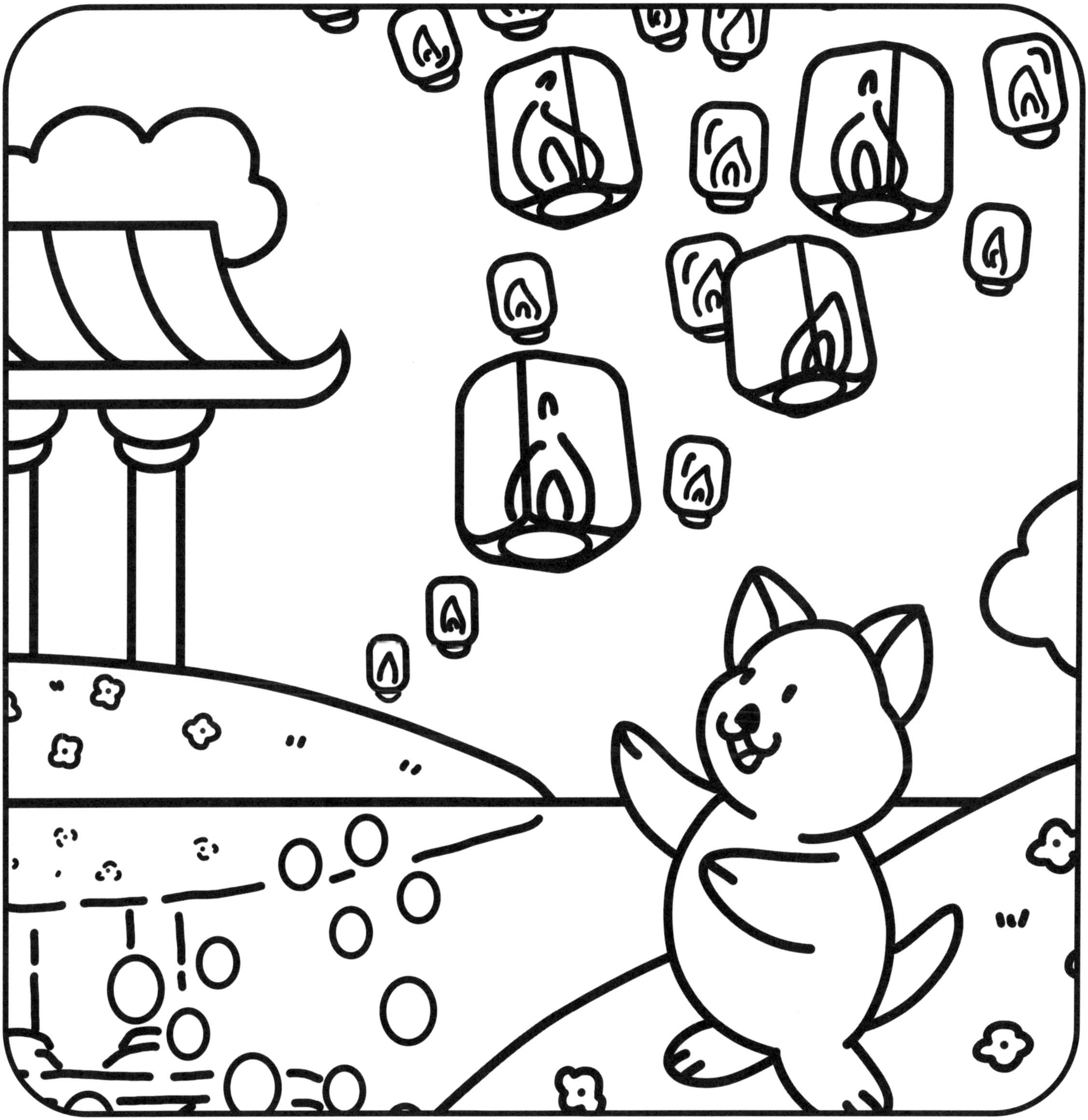

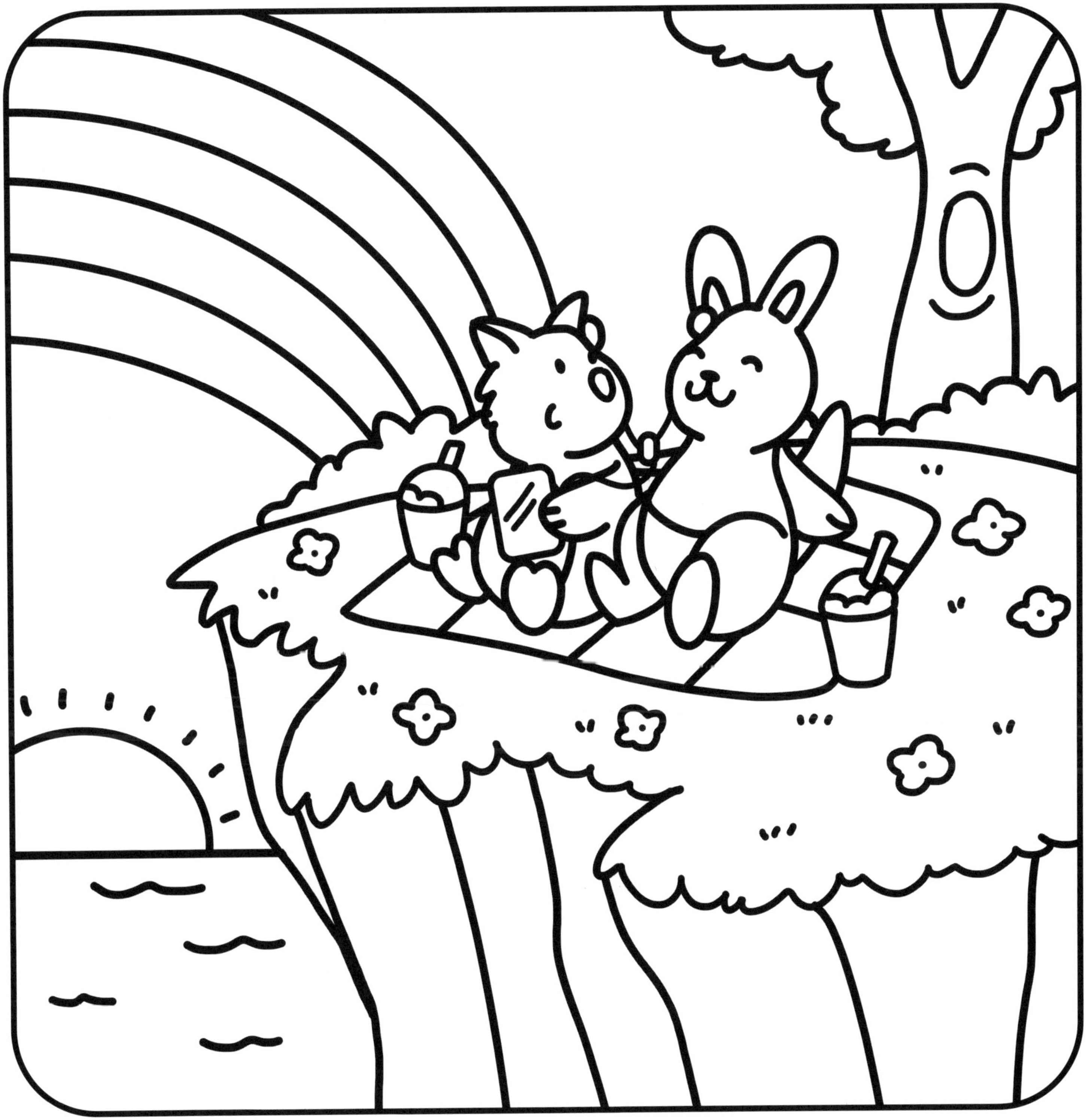